METAVERSE

COMPLETE GUIDE - 2022 & Beyond

**"An investment in knowledge
pays the best interest"**

- Benjamin Franklin.

METAVERSE INVESTING

ULTIMATE GUIDE

The Meta-Verse

ABOUT THE AUTHOR

The Meta-Verse

The Meta-Verse are researchers
Based in London, England.

The Meta-Verse is a collective; we
work with the most senior
academic researchers, writers and
knowledge makers.

**We are in the changing
lives business.**

JOIN OUR

NFT, CRYPTO ART, METAVERSE & DEFI

Entrepreneur Power Group

To help reinforce the learning's from our books, I strongly suggest you join our well-informed powerhouse community on Facebook.

Here, you will connect and share with other like-minded people to support your journey and help you grow.

>>>CLICK BELOW to join Our NFT Group <<<

News Site & Community Group:

https://www.facebook.com/groups/nfttrending/

Want Future Book Releases?

Email us at:

<u>mindsetmastership@gmail.com</u>

Find us on Instagram!

@MindsetMastership

MASTERSHIP BOOKS

UK | USA | Canada | Ireland | Australia

India | New Zealand | South Africa | China

Mastership Books is part of the United Arts Publishing House group of companies based in London, England, UK.

First published by Mastership Books (London, UK), 2022

I S B N: 978-1-915002-13-6

Text Copyright © United Arts Publishing

Cover design by Rich © United Arts Publishing (UK)

Text and internal design by Rich © United Arts Publishing (UK)

Image credits reserved.

Colour separation by Spitting Image Design Studio

Printed and bound in Great Britain

National Publications Association of Britain

London, England, United Kingdom.

Paper design UAP

ISBN: 978-1-915002-13-6

(paperback)

A723.5

Title: **Metaverse Investing Ultimate Guide**

Design, Bound & Printed:

London, England,
Great Britain.

THE METAVERSE COMPLETE GUIDE

"If you really want to invest in something today, start investing in **NFTs**, **Metaverse** and **Domains**, these hidden treasure and going mainstream"

CONTENTS:

JOIN OUR

FIRST READER REVIEW

TEAM

HERE:

mindsetmastership@gmail.com

0

INTRODUCTION

Second Life Vs. Metaverse

The metaverse, a virtual environment where millions of individuals might soon converge to work, play, and socialize, is causing quite a stir in the tech industry. The concept, however, is not as novel as it may appear. Since 2003, individuals have gathered in the online environment of Second Life to perform all of the above activities.

Second Life's founders, Linden Lab, underline that second life is not a game, unlike other proto-metaverse experiences like Fortnite or Roblox. In the second life. Participants design a digital avatar to represent themselves and explore the environment, meet other users, develop their unique digital content, and even exchange products and services in-world currencies, the Linden Dollar.

Second Life peaked in the late 2000s. Its keyboard and mouse controls and blocky visuals are far from the refined vision of immersive environments broadcast via virtual reality headsets that corporations like Meta and Microsoft are pushing. Second Life, on the other hand, continues to have a loyal fan base and is perhaps the longest-running experiment in the potential of a metaverse-like world.

There are two recent events that are not directly related to metaverse technological growth but have led to the popularity of the metaverse. One is COVID, where there has been concern that we may have to relocate certain social and leisure activities online. Many major corporations are attempting to figure out how to profit from this. The other is merely Meta's argument that it is a big deal and rebranding themselves to attempt to align with it.

It is worth noting that Second Life is still the largest and closest approach to a metaverse that we have for adults. The settings utilized by children, like Roblox, are also quite engaging, but they provide different experiences. If you talk about individuals wanting to go to a live concert or go shopping or something like that, the Second Life is worth $650 million in transactions each year and has a million users. However, Second Life never grew beyond a million users. Due to the pandemic, it has grown a slightly bigger user base, and it has not broken out into the mainstream. However, Meta (previously Facebook) hopes that a billion individuals will use their new metaverse.

The reason the second life did not succeed, and this is still the case today, is that most adults are not yet comfortable dealing with new individuals or participating socially in a multi-player environment online. It has been quite gratifying for those who have benefited from this. There have been works even with High Fidelity, a whole VR experience. However, with headgear rather than desktop—there are still only a tiny group of individuals who have enjoyed the platform or chance to earn money, and other things, from the Second Life game.

However, they are not suitable for everyone. People cannot communicate effectively through facial expressions or proper body language, which takes too much effort to imagine. If you have the option of having your social life take place in the actual world, the vast majority of people will choose that option, and it is a binary decision. They do not divide their social lives between the actual world and the virtual world. That is why we have not seen the breakout yet, and nothing Meta has said or proven alters my opinion.

We are witnessing specific industry prospects with the metaverse, such as collaborative brainstorming and design. There are innovative ways for individuals to use virtual reality to hold effective long-distance meetings.

There are several questions to be answered to achieve anything resembling the scale of the Internet. If you want to develop a multi-billion-dollar virtual world, everyone will have to work in tandem. The idea that all of those niches might be filled by a single corporation like Meta, Google, or Apple seems unrealistic.

Another thing we need is digital money so that people may trade. A money system that transcends numerous local currencies is required to create metaverse systems in which one person may build a car and sell it to many others. However, to some extent, we have that with cryptocurrencies.

We are completely focused on spatial audio right now since it is a profitable and rapidly developing industry. The capacity to simultaneously produce high-quality 3D audio for a large group of individuals is vital to this technology. We also think it is progressive; it is a feasible project that we can get started on. We have been thrilled about every aspect of this, but we believe that audio is the most important fundamental component that everyone will require. We will keep looking at it and figuring out what unfolds next, and contributing as thinkers and leaders in the sector.

The reinvention of the Second Life

Second Life used to be a popular virtual world before it experienced a loss of public attention. However, Second Life's inventor, Philip Rosedale, has chosen to appoint a core team to improve Second Life now that the metaverse has gained a tremendous focus of attention. He expects that the development of community-focused environments such as Second Life will address some metaverse concerns that are not necessarily being addressed in VR headsets right now.

Rosedale plans to be the "strategic adviser" for Second Life. At the same time, his business, High Fidelity tries to inject Second Life with fresh ideas while also exploring other modern tech concepts, including VR. They plan to announce the transfer of seven personnel, certain patents, and some funds. They want to invest in Second Life to keep working on it. Two patents are for moderation in a decentralized system, which is pretty amazing.

According to them, the Second Life is still profitable and has a far larger population than other VR platforms: over 73 million accounts have been generated since its inception, with estimates of active users hovering around 900,000. They view the transition as a solution to challenges while VR gear is still being developed.

They envision Second Life evolving into a better platform that will remain VR-optional until that mysteriously flawless hardware emerges. However, even the finest virtual environment, such as Second Life, are still somewhat constrained. Second Life allows you to gather up to 100 people in one location simultaneously. That is not enough, but it is more than all the other platforms combined regarding people standing around. They want Second Life to be more decentralized but admit it is a difficult balance to strike.

Virtual audio might be included in this new version, but more complex avatar animations may be based on facial detection through cameras: Using the camera to animate an avatar is a pretty intriguing in-between. There are not many people looking at that area. Credit to their team for spending a lot of time thinking about it. Also, they are thinking about how Second Life may operate on phones in the future.

Development to Reshape Second Life, Metaverse and Virtual Economies

Tilia Pay

Tilia Pay may fuel virtual economies in many industries as they try to entice consumers to come in and invest money in their edition of the metaverse and then enable individuals to cash out their digital profits. It is a fundamental role of the metaverse, and Second Life has been doing it for a long time.

This is not as simple as it appears. Platform publishers would first adhere to money transfer restrictions to pay authors for their virtual content. Because when money is exchanged for virtual products and cashed out by artists, the platform publisher becomes a money transmitter and licensed. This is also true for exchanges that trade NFTs.

Tilia is the only licensed and insured money transmitter focusing on cryptocurrency, gaming, and NFT. Tilia Pay, which provides "financial rails" for publishers, functions as a hybrid of PayPal and Coinbase for virtual environments and gaming sites. Virtual environments, games, publishers, and non-fungible tokens exchanges may lawfully enable creators and others to convert cryptocurrency into cash using their Tilia wallets.

Upland, an NFT-based digital property trading environment where people may play a form of Monopoly by purchasing, selling, and trading virtual assets tied to real-world locations, is one of the new Tilia customers. Before its agreement with Tilia, Upland users could not sell their virtual assets to other players for US dollars since allowing financial transfers from one user to another necessitated money transmitter licenses in the US and other countries. Tilia stepped in to help, and Upland now has over 100,000 monthly active users.

Zenescope

Other initiatives are also taking place in Second Life to pique user interest. It partnered with comic book publisher Zenescope Entertainment and licensing agency Epik to bring the dark and twisted Grimm's Universe to reality as the Zenescope Metaverse within Second Life.

Interacting with and acting as some of the iconic fairy tale characters popularized by Zenescope's comic books and graphic novels, fans may act out events and adopt different narratives. Cinderella (aka Cindy): Serial Killer Princess, the main heroine of a six-issue miniseries of the same name, is featured in the virtual experience. Belle, the Beast Hunter, the Mad Hatter, and Jabberwocky are also present. Zenescope fans reach approximately 70 million, and they now have up to 50 different digital items to purchase within the Second Life environment. According to Oberwager, this is only the start of several new brand and entertainment partner engagements in Second Life. At the moment, metaverses are all the rage. Second Life was a pioneer, but many people are unaware that it is still alive and well.

1

METAVERSE VIRTUAL REALITY PRODUCT INVESTMENT

Metaverse Future Products and Applications

Introduction

Consider climbing Everest, swimming with sharks, or flying over the Grand Canyon within the four walls of your living room. According to tech experts, all of these will be achievable in the metaverse. In its completely developed form, the metaverse promises to provide real-life experiences, sounds and even smells, allowing you to go on a journey of ancient Greece or visit a Seoul café from the comfort of your own home.

You would not even need to be yourself. Participants of the metaverse may roam the Brazilian amazon like a jaguar or hit the floor as LeBron James at Madison Square Garden, and your imagination is the only barrier. The metaverse will produce a tailored and augmented reality for each individual using a mix of physical and behavioral biometrics, emotion detection, sentiment analysis, and personal data.

Metaverse Products

In the future, augmented reality wearables may be as prevalent as smartphones are now. We envision a future in which headsets such as the Oculus, a popular holiday gift this season that welcomes you to "defy reality," completely replace the smartphone. Also, it will serve as a regular device for individuals to socialize with friends, shop, or take trips through virtual environments 24 hours a day, seven days a week. Like Snap, Amazon, Microsoft, and Mark Zuckerberg's Meta, several firms have competing interpretations of this new digital universe.

Certain parts of the future metaverse are already taking shape.

Metaverse Applications for Artists

Music artists have adopted virtual reality through "Fortnite," a streaming and cosplay-friendly game in which avatars assemble on a mythical island in large numbers.

Ariana Grande started her "Rift" tour on August 6 with a virtual performance on the free-to-play game. Her anime alter ego dressed in a frock made of broken glass bits and wielding a gigantic crystal hammer. The songs were pre-recorded. However, viewers could see Grande sing and dance while swishing her signature ponytail.

You might even purchase and wear her "skin" - the star's simulated appearance — as your avatar. She allegedly divided the revenues from in-game sales with the show's designer, Epic Games, and earned a nice $20 million. Since its first release in 2017, the game has made over $10 billion in revenue.

Possibilities for Cities and Landscapes

According to the Seoul Metropolitan Government, Seoul became the first city to declare ambitions to go completely meta. The government stated that it would develop a fully realized virtual "environment for all aspects of its municipal government, like economic, cultural, tourism, educational, and civic service.

The agency stated that its most famous tourist destinations would be reproduced in a virtual environment on a platform it intends to debut in 2023. They plan to be a unified system. However, "Having global standards that support this is critical.

They envision a landscape where they can buy virtual clothing in world A and wear it in world B. Since the metaverse typically includes physical activity — whether chasing aliens or attending a yoga class — it also brings real-life advantages. Luxury businesses are attempting to match the demand for jazzing up avatars by making virtual clothing you will never wear and shoes you cannot put on your real-life feet. And no demographic is overlooked.

Clothing Products

Ralph Lauren is selling beanies and down coats for the elementary school set on Roblox, a cartoon-like game with 150 million players and a $38 billion valuation.

Gucci, Balenciaga, and Dior have launched collections targeting Gen Z gamers, including high-end designer clothes, purses, and accessories. On December 13, Nike purchased RTFKT, a digital sneaker startup that sold 600 pairs of shoes and generated $3 million – all without building a single pair.

Hermès, the brand behind the insanely costly Birkin bag, has also joined the metaverse. On December 17, the firm debuted the MetaBirkin, a virtual reality replica of its distinctive bag designed by LA artist Mason Rothschild and limited to 100 pieces. Because there is a scarcity, prices have soared dramatically. The price for a bag is now approaching real Birkin values, with some going for as much as £40,000.

Medical and Military Products

Doctors are also fully utilizing modern technology. Before performing any surgeries, surgical residents at UConn Health put on Oculus headsets and practice procedures in virtual reality, inserting pins in simulated shattered bones and learning from experience.

Neurosurgeons now use virtual reality during a spinal fusion procedure while wearing Augmedics headsets, which contain a "laser eye display that projected visuals of a patient's interior anatomies, like bones and other internal tissue.

Holographic graphics and virtual reality technologies are now being used to guide first responders in treating heart attack patients. Military veterans are learning to cure their own PTSD by donning a headset and, with the help of a therapist, returning to the time they were wounded or traumatized on the war front.

Plastic surgery will also become less of a gamble. Rather than asking the patient to imagine what the alterations would look like, surgeons will employ digital twin technologies, synthetic media, haptics, and robotics to show and enable the patient to touch the alterations. 'How do you like your new nose?'

Tech Giants New VR Products

According to Wall Street, many businesses and tech behemoths are already developing the technology and software to power the next generation of virtual contact – a $1 trillion industry. Google, Microsoft, Apple, Valve, and more corporations develop solutions for work and communication. As investors rush into the sector, smaller firms are likely to join them due to their immense potential. We have provided a list of some prominent tech giants whose products Meta will have to fight with as it attempts to establish its presence in the meta-landscape.

Project Cambria (Meta Quest Pro)

Project Cambria, previously called Oculus Quest Pro, is Meta's new high-end virtual reality headset. The project is still in progress and will most likely debut at the company's Connect event (a virtual reality showcase) in 2022. This new virtual reality headset is a high-end Oculus virtual reality headsets model, not a successor to Quest 2. Some leaked instructional videos also reveal the device's appearance (similar to the new HTC Vive Flow).

Face tracking and real-color passthrough are some of the features that will be included in the headset. A real-color passthrough will transform the headset into a true Mixed Reality (XR) device that can run virtual and augmented reality apps. Unfortunately, the company did not provide any other details on the new VR headset.

HTC Vive Flow

HTC Vive Flow, the company's newest standalone virtual reality headset, has finally been released. According to the company, the headset is designed basically for media applications and casual gaming. It will not come with any controls, so we will have to use smartphones to operate it. The headset will include 6 degree of freedom (FOD) head tracking and can be used as a 3DOF controller with an Android smartphone.

The headset costs around $499, making it more expensive than the Oculus Quest 2. When it comes to virtual reality headsets, the specifications are not the best. Although more expensive, it is driven by Snapdragon XR1, which is less effective than the XR2 in the Oculus Quest 2.

An external power supply, such as your smartphone or a battery pack, is also required. Nevertheless, the headset will come with adaptive diopter lenses that enable up to -6.0D focusing power, which is great news for folks who wear prescription lenses.

Project Galea and Valve Index 2 (Deckard)

Valve is also developing a new virtual reality headset on the Valve Index 2, codenamed Deckard. Like Oculus Quest 2, it will be a standalone virtual reality headset. According to Valve's latest patents, the gadget appears modular, allowing for future updates and attachments. Most of this material comes from YouTuber Brad Lynch, who has discovered a wealth of information and patents on the headset.

On the other hand, Project Galea is a virtual reality headset that individuals may control directly with their minds. Valve, OpenBCI, and

Tobii are currently researching it for useful applications. The project is expected to begin early in 2022, although it appears limited to developers. Even so, initiatives like these yield tremendous results in the long run.

PSVR 2

Sony has officially announced that the PSVR 2 will be released. Recently, the PlayStation blog introduced the company's new PSVR technology, which is now in development. Since then, patents and insider leaks have verified new facts concerning the virtual reality headset. The field of view, display quality, and controls of PSVR 2 will all be significantly improved.

In terms release date, rumors indicate that PSVR 2 would be released during the Christmas season of 2022, according to insider information. The headset will include backward compatibility and new capabilities like eye-tracking and Wi-Fi. In terms of content, Sony appears to be focusing on AAA virtual reality titles for its virtual world, which means more PSVR-only games.

Panasonic MeganeX VR Headset

Panasonic unveiled MeganeX, a lightweight, small virtual reality headset that measures over eight ounces, making it far lighter than existing headsets. The headset will run SteamVR apps, a VR content platform accessible on rival headsets like the HTC Vive and Oculus. The MeganeX also has a foldable frame with speakers integrated into it.

The headset's architecture solves one of the barriers to mass virtual reality adoption: the size of current headsets. To be broadly accepted by customers, virtual reality headsets must be lightweight and comfortable to use and produce lifelike pictures. Panasonic did not say when the device would be available or whether it would work without being directly linked to a computer.

Virtual Reality Headsets from other Manufacturers

Varjo, Decagear, and Pimax have all showcased new and future virtual reality headsets. Although many of these firms are not as large as the ones listed above, the headsets they sell are rather advanced. Despite their high prices, the Varjo XR-3 and Pimax Reality are presently the most sophisticated virtual reality headsets. Many more firms are following suit and building their virtual and augmented reality headsets. This is all only a prelude to the development of the Metaverse.

Marrying the Digital and Physical Worlds

Though businesses are finding value in solely digital products such as NFTs, physical products for sector-specific applications, and in-game fashion, the actual sweet spot for the marketing items market may be at the crossroads of physical and virtual products.

For instance, in preparation for a virtual event or trade fair, a business may send out a pair of branded socks or another item. The receiver might then be directed to a location where they could buy or acquire an NFT of the digital edition of the socks that they could then wear at the virtual event through a QR code on the box. The exciting thing about this is that our business loses so much money on goods that are thrown away, and this technology eliminates it. We can be both sustainable and effective by combining the physical and virtual products we offer."

The transaction might also occur in the reverse direction, with a person purchasing an NFT, which subsequently "unlocks" real-world items and experiences. When NFTs are acquired using crypto, they become an immutable blockchain component, and it unlocks everything you tell it to.

Kings of Leon became the first band to release an album as an NFT, and part of the release featured an auction of six "Golden Tickets," each of which guarantees the holder four front-row tickets at all Kings of Leon headline tour for the rest of their lives. According to Adidas, the 30,000

NFTs issued last year will be linked to genuine tangible stuff that token owners would be able to redeem for free in 2022.

Barker and Fosdick's cryptocurrency company, NFTs4Charity, likewise explores unlockable content. The Elizabeth Glaser Pediatric AIDS Foundation, founded by the late widow of Starsky & Hutch star Paul Michael Glaser, coordinated a non-fungible token auction with the firm. Trish Classe Gianakis, a digital artist, was commissioned by Glaser to produce two works of art that would be simulated and turned into NFTs. Winners of the auction would get a physical copy of the virtual artwork, customized and signed by Glaser; a private mobile or Zoom discussion with Glaser; a customized and signed version of a book written by Glaser; a package of memorable clothing and accessories; and a vintage, circa the 1970s customized and signed photo of Glaser as Det. Starsky.

Metaverse Wearables and Accessories

The metaverse will be nothing more than a pipedream without wearable technologies to connect the physical and virtual environments. The metaverse's entire premise is to virtually experience realism. Virtual reality with wearables supporting the immersive experience is the only way to achieve it.

Virtual glasses are the most critical instrument for any metaverse or augmented reality experience. Virtual reality glasses have been around for a while. While there have been various applications in gaming and manufacturing, virtual reality glasses are set to transform the metaverse's overall experience.

In reality, the tech industry is already employing wearable equipment with sensors that gather data and provide feedback to users. Industrial wearables are not the same as wearables built for immersive experiences in virtual public environments like the metaverse, despite the similarities in technology. However, while virtual reality headsets allow one to enjoy the metaverse, the experience is not as full as one might want. Gamers wore sensor suits to get the full immersive experience. These outfits are designed to mirror the metaverse's virtual environment. The suit, for instance, would make a player feel cold if they were in a cold region in the metaverse.

Haptic Gloves

One such item designed for the metaverse is the haptic glove. It is not Thanos' glove but rather Zuckerberg's preferred hand sock. The glove, created by Meta Reality Labs, allows participants to interact with virtual items in the metaverse by touching and feeling them. A person interacting with a virtual animal in the metaverse, for instance, could be able to feel its texture when they brush their palm against it.

The significance of hands in overcoming the interface challenge in augmented and virtual reality is immersive. We need our hands to interact with one another, learn about the environment, and act in it. If we can bring complete hand involvement into augmented and virtual reality, we can reap the benefits of a decade of motor learning. People may engage with virtual items in the same way they interact with actual objects, without learning a new method of dealing with the environment.

The goal is to create portable haptic gloves that handle both sides of the augmented and virtual reality interaction challenge, in this example, assisting the computer in understanding and reflecting a user's hand movements while also simulating the feeling and experience. The gloves would need to be fashionable, comfortable, affordable, robust, and adjustable for the product to be effective. To put it another way, they would have to connect to the virtual reality headset.

To provide a genuine feeling of touch, haptic gloves require hundreds of actuators (small motors) distributed all over the hand, all working in harmony to give the user the sensation of holding a virtual item. Researchers are thrilled and looking forward to the outcome of the haptic glove and its influence on the metaverse once it is ready, even though research is still underway.

Wearable Skins

Tech companies are similarly working on a wearable sensory suit in addition to the haptic glove. The suit resembles a skin referred to as Reskin, which includes magnetic particles within that generate a magnetic field, similar to the fictional haptic suit in Ready Player One.

Scientists from Carnegie Melon University and Meta AI researchers work together to build the skin. The skin is made of flexible plastic and is just around 3mm thick. The magnetic field from the implanted particles varies when the skin collides with another surface. The sensor monitors the difference in magnetic flux before transmitting the information to artificial intelligence algorithms that try to figure out what force or touch was applied.

Reskin might be used in robotic hands, prosthetic limbs, or smart wearables such as gloves that enable an individual to sense what another is touching. For quick manipulation activities like sliding, tossing, catching, and clapping, ReSkin can also give high-frequency three-axis tactile signals. It may also be readily removed and replaced as it wears out.

A universal tactile sensing skin such as ReSkin will offer a rich source of contact data that might aid the development of AI in a wide range of touch-based activities, such as object recognition, proprioception, and robotic grasping. AI models with learnt tactile sensing capabilities will be capable of a wide range of jobs, including those requiring more sensitivity, like working in health-care environments, or better skill, such as manipulating small, soft, or delicate things. It is unclear how or when the skins will be accessible for people to try out in the metaverse. However, given the amount of research and development that has gone into the project, it is only a matter of time until this metaverse wearable is released.

Virtual and Augmented Reality Accessories Categories

Virtual and augmented reality customized and purpose-built

accessories may appear to be niche products. Despite this, their development, manufacture, and distribution continue to grow rapidly. As a result, there is certainly a demand for these items.

Virtual Reality and Augmented Reality Accessories for Gaming

The newest extended reality hardware devices make their debut in the gaming world. Gaming is a great incubator for VR/AR products that add just one more minor layer of authenticity to immersive environments, thanks to the raw creativity of designing exclusively for entertainment purposes.

Nintendo Labo VR

In the future, there is no doubt that young Switch owners worldwide will be fantasizing about Nintendo's new VR gear. Labo blends downloadable updates for popular Switch games with DIY cardboard additions to provide a unique gaming experience.

Five Tilt

The old-school role-playing game format receives an augmented reality boost with this holographic tabletop technology. Irrespective of how we categorize it, this device is just too fantastic to overlook, even if it is not an accessory. Augmented reality glasses, a holographic gaming board, and a wand that allows interaction make up the system.

Cybershoes

These shoes look to be both intriguing and challenging. As a result, we are curious to see where this technology goes. The bottoms of your feet are turned into smart data-gathering devices thanks to a brilliant mix of sensors and electronics. The requirement to stay sitting while wearing the shoes, on the other hand, places a hard limit on how realistic the present configuration will seem.

MAG P90 Gun

Regardless of your feelings on violent entertainment, the first-person shooter genre is booming alongside the virtual reality business. Fans of Halo, Call of Duty, and John Wick are likely to be eager to get their hands on one of these guns and embark on an adrenaline-fueled adventure.

Virtual and Augmented Reality Personal Accessories

Sensoryx VR Free Gloves

Thanks to their fingertipless design and headset mount companion piece, these gloves are comfortable and effective. They can track 3D hands and fingers. Gloves, in general, provide a greater range of motion than controllers, making them seem more natural. And the Sensoryx gloves clearly state that they "return hands to VR users."

Feelreal Sensory Mask

The capacity to smell in a virtual environment appears to go under the radar in product priority areas. Smell is a delicate component of everyday life, but it is essential for genuine immersion in particular locations, such as the tropics. This mask also produces mist and wind, giving you more bang for your buck.

Location-based Virtual and Augmented Reality Accessories

Immersive arcades and virtual reality lounges are springing up worldwide, bringing with them the chance to try out high-end virtual reality gear. The consumer base is expanding, from business teambuilding events to birthdays and bachelor events. With that expansion, we may expect to see more advanced virtual and augmented reality accessories that are not intended for household usage.

Roto VR Chair

When it comes to making a virtual environment feel real, full physical immersion goes a long way. Being seated also eliminates the need for heavy connections and the stress of moving safely. This motorized chair ticks many boxes for consumers interested in flying or driving simulators and space habitats, and airborne adventures. Even though the

Roto chair is not completely confined to arcade or storefront environments, its almost $2,000 price tag and big size make it unsuitable for casual home users.

Aperium K-01 Treadmill

Although this treadmill is exclusively a business item, we are pleased to see developments like this made available to retail outlets. The K-01 walking surface employs a V-Orient system to naturally accelerate and decelerate while readjusting the virtual environment as needed.

Vortx Whirlwind FX

It may seem easy to add a little wind or heat to an interactive experience, but consider what it takes to synchronize such elements with the game's action. The Vortx achieves exactly that, and like the Roto chair, it can be used at home by virtual reality devotees.

The majority of these (and similar) game-oriented products (and others) may be combined into experiences that your company can utilize. Making your virtual world as realistic as feasible boosts your outcomes, regardless of what you require.

Future Technologies

Extensive Gameplay

First and foremost, it is time to lighten the mood after the last two years. Gaming is becoming increasingly engaging, intending to immerse the user more deeply in the game's universe. Sony revealed details about their next-generation VR console for the PlayStation 5. The new console will include an improved eye-tracking technology that detects user eye movement. Gamers may now look from side to side rather than fully twisting their heads to explore their environments, giving the game character more realistic input. This results in a more interactive experience since the gamer may behave intuitively, just as they would in real life, with a heightened emotional reaction and increased expressiveness, bringing gaming to a new level of realism.

When the games are over, VR may be utilized to run long-distance meetings while still retaining the benefits of face-to-face meetings. Shiftall, a Panasonic subsidiary, showcased many new items at CES 2022 aimed at assisting users in immersing themselves in the metaverse,

Luxury Jewellery

What would a wearable item be if it did not have a fitness tracker? The Circular Ring is a definite upgrade from watches. This ring, which will be unveiled at CES 2022, examines the user's bio-signals 24/7 to monitor their health trends. It can measure blood oxygenation and heart rate to a clinical level by mixing red and infrared light.

Overall, health must maintain a proper balance of oxygen-saturated blood. A normal value is between 94 and 100 percent; any excess or too little might be harmful. This is an important statistic to track since it is linked to many respiratory problems (shortness of breath, asthma, sleep apnea, and more). Monitoring blood oxygen levels may aid in different tasks, including detecting and preventing certain diseases and evaluating whether treatments are effective. Owners may use this ring to discover what factors influence their health and how they impact their days.

Wearables offer tremendous money-making opportunities for tech companies and investors. Below are popular metaverse wearables tech companies with promising stocks for investors.

Unity

Unity is well-known as a game engine that enables the creation of games and gaming materials. However, it is likely the firm with the most partnerships with VR companies, maybe even more than the major VR companies, to design different categories of metaverse wearables.

iTechArt Group

iTechArt Group is a leading software development firm that assists businesses in reshaping their solutions via augmented and interactive experiences. iTechArt's teams produce strong sector-specific AR and VR solutions incorporating AI, IoT, blockchain, and other robust technologies.

Oculus

Oculus is well renowned for being the first company to create a contemporary virtual reality headset and represent a promising stock for investment.

HTC

HTC is a company that makes more than only smartphones and other electronic gadgets. After the initial professional HTC Vive headset was introduced in 2017, they developed the first institutional-grade VR headset HTC Vive Pro and two further variants of the Pro Eye.

Samsung

Their first branded smartphone-based VR experience, the Samsung Gear VR, was likely the first low-cost alternative for mid-range VR experiences to go mainstream. It is now a more desirable alternative for individuals who wish to avoid the more expensive solutions.

Microsoft

Microsoft is popular for its computer, IoT, and networking products, but it is famous for its augmented reality (AR) projects like the Windows HoloLens and Windows Holographic development platform.

VironIT

VironIT specializes in mobile, web-based, and enterprise software apps and software support, maintenance, and integration. It also covers the Internet of Things, robots, and blockchain development.

Next//Now

Next/Now is a VR and AR design company that works on applications, animations, fairs, trade exhibitions, and festivals. It is also investing massively in the metaverse wearable.

Quyttech

Quyttech is an Indian VR and artificial intelligence company that works with HTC Vive, Oculus, HoloLens, and other platforms.

2

VIRTUAL LAND AS NFTS

It is no secret that the real estate market is booming. Certainly, some investors are spending millions of dollars for parcels of land, not in New York or Beverly Hills. In reality, the land does not exist in the real world, and rather, the plot is found on the metaverse. Prices for plots have risen by up to 500 percent in recent months, following Meta's announcement that it was going all-in on VR, even changing its business name.

A tract of digital real estate represented by NFT is called NFT metaverse land. Depending on the platform, the owner can utilize their property for socializing, marketing, work, gaming, and other purposes. Cryptocurrency is commonly used to monetize transactions in the virtual environment. Non-fungible tokens (NFTs), rather than cryptos, are the principal means of monetizing and trading value inside the metaverse.

You can purchase NFT metaverse land via a project's land sale or by using an NFT marketplace platform to purchase directly from owners. To acquire the land, you will need a digital wallet and cryptocurrency. Land may also be sold to other users on various sites, and renting methods will be accessible in the future.

An NFT is a one-of-a-kind digital asset. Although NFTs are generally works of digital art (such as films, photographs, music, or 3D objects), an NFT can include a wide range of assets, including virtual real estate. There are already parcels of land or even virtual residences on OpenSea, where individuals buy and exchange NFTs.

However, to maintain the value of the virtual real estate, supply must be controlled — a notion known in economics as "scarcity value." Decentraland, for instance, is made up of 90,000 plots of land, or "parcels," typically around 50 feet by 50 feet.

We are already witnessing instances where the value of the virtual real estate is increasing.

Virtual Land Current Acquisitions

Republic Realm, a virtual real estate investment fund, allegedly committed more than US$900,000 in June 2021 to purchase an NFT reflecting a parcel on Decentraland. According to DappRadar, a website that records NFT sales statistics, it was the costliest purchase of NFT land in Decentraland history.

In November 2021, the Metaverse Group paid US$2.4 million for their plot in Decentraland. This acquisition was less than the previous one - 116 land parcels vs 259 purchased by Republic Realm. It is not just Decentraland that is enjoying a rise in popularity. Axie Infinity (another digital game world) allegedly sold nine of its land pieces for the equivalent of US$1.5 million in February 2021.

PwC is one of the most recent entrants, having paid an unknown sum for real estate in The Sandbox, a virtual game environment. In the metaverse, there are regions where people congregate. According to experts, these locations will be more valuable than locations where no events occur.

To be sure, those high-traffic zones attract big spenders. Consider the board game Monopoly. Location s where people gather is significantly more important for advertising and merchants to develop ways to access that audience.

Snoop Dogg, for instance, is constructing a virtual house on a parcel of land in Sandbox, and someone recently offered $450,000 to be his neighbor. It is important who your neighbor is, which is nearly true for practically everything. It is like a club, so you want to hang out with others with similar interests. Purchasing virtual land is straightforward, whether done directly via the platform or a developer. Entrepreneurs can create interactive structures on their plots. You may decorate it, modify it, and renovate it as much as you like.

However, virtual land real estate is very risky; hence, you should only invest money you are willing to lose, much like the traditional cryptocurrency investment. However, it is speculative; it can be extremely lucrative.

Factors that Affect the Value of Land

Since every parcel is an NFT, each has its distinct token ID. However, like with real-world property, some key factors determine what individuals are prepared to pay for. Knowing these is critical to understanding the Metaverse's underpinning economy; therefore, let us go through the essential points to note here:

- **Purpose of the land**

Land may be solely an investment for landowners. However, for anything more particular, such as creating a digital experience, whether or not a parcel of land has the necessary features will be critical to its value.

- **The land growth potential**

Measuring this entails examining the existing use cases, which businesses are available on the platform and the project's market capitalization.

- **The location and specific qualities of the land**

As briefed earlier, the location of the land will be crucial to its value. Is the surrounding neighborhood appealing for your application and in line with your goals?

- **The plot Accessibility**

Like any property, accessibility is critical to its value, and buyers in the Metaverse should consider this by searching on the native map to get a notion of where your possible new property is.

- **Scarcity**

Yes, supply and demand have a globally recognized effect anytime something is purchased or sold, and the Metaverse is no exception. The availability of comparable parcels of land will significantly influence what is offered.

- **The value of the underlining token/floor price**

Because each Metaverse has its unique token that will be used to acquire land right from the platform, the value of this token is an important driver of pricing for primary sales. When buying on the secondary market, the floor price of land — that is, the absolute lowest price at which you may join the project at any given time – will decide how much purchasers are ready to spend across the board.

Sandbox Land

Sandbox is a decentralized community-driven game environment where creators and artists can develop, distribute, and sell their assets as NFTs. Furthermore, gaming experiences on the Ethereum blockchain and Sandbox have teamed with major industry titans such as Square Enix and Atari. Sandbox is renowned for virtual real estate taking over the NFT sector.

Land may be developed and monetized by its owners. A set of neighboring property can be combined to form an estate, giving the owner access to a greater area for development. Lands are a limited resource in the Sandbox Metaverse, with just 166,464 accessible in total. Owning land in the Sandbox provides its holders with several options. Land's major job is to host and play activities like games, galleries, social centers, and so on. And the owner may monetize all of this as a source of revenue. Sandbox's governance token is Sand, and owners will receive intriguing incentives.

Benefits of Sandbox Land to Investors

Having a parcel of virtual real estate known as lands on the Sandbox will offer you several options to create a very clean and consistent source of revenue. Let us go through how land may make you very wealthy in the Sandbox.

Hosting Experience

Property on Sandbox's major role is to enable owners to host live experiences like games, art museums, stores, sceneries, interactive education, and so on. These experiences may be planned and built with Sandbox's unique game development tools, known as the Game Maker, and then released on any developer's properties. Players may have to pay an entry fee in crypto to access the experience offered on the land.

Staking

A potential Sandbox feature will allow owners to stake cryptocurrencies on their properties in return for passive benefits. One of these benefits is GEMs, an ERC-20 token that is extremely coveted and sought after by property creation specialists. In addition to the standard staking incentives, these GEMs may be traded on the market. The number of Land parcels you own functions as a multiplier when you deliver SAND-ETH cash flow to the UniSwap liquidity provider, increasing the amount of SAND token you earn through cash flow mining.

Renting

Landowners can rent out their lands to others, like game developers and film production businesses that lost out on land during the initial auction. Once all of the lands have been sold, the amount of available land for rent will surge as more individuals become aware of The Sandbox and opt to create an experience there.

Host Contests and Giveaways

Lands can host events and contests, drawing a sizable number of paying users to your property to participate in the contest or giveaway. You might also enable others to hold competitions or raffles on your lands to promote their businesses — for a price, of course.

Self-Promotion Ads and Affiliate Linking

Are you a true affiliate? Do you own a company? Are you a writer? Are you a professional artist? Or anyone looking to market a product or service? Why not widen your reach by utilizing part of your advertising space on your land to market yourself to players and visitors who might otherwise be ignorant of the product of your commodity or service?

Selling Asset NFTs

If you decide to publish an experience on your property, you will need to set up entry criteria and charge a price to access the experience. One of the entry criteria you might set is that participants hold a certain asset NFT. For example, a gamer may acquire a sword from an NFT sword set you released on the public market to enjoy a swashbuckling pirate game you released on the property.

Selling Land

Selling land inside the platform is another way to generate money, especially in a high-traffic and highly prized area of the Metaverse. Suppose you peacefully hang onto your property for a lengthier period. In that case, you will most probably earn more money in the future through a combination of the various strategies listed above.

Buying Land in the Sandbox Environment

To acquire a Sandbox land, you must first set up an account, the most apparent step. The signup process may only take a couple of minutes. And in this case, we are utilizing Metamask, the most common wallet. As a result, you must first establish a Metamask account and then download the Metamask browser plugin.

You may create a Metamask account and get the improved version from their official website. After installing Metamask, go to Sandbox's website and click the sign-in icon in the upper right corner of the page. Choose Metamask from the drop-down option. Following that, you will be asked to provide an email address and a user ID. Then, simply click the Create an Account button, and you are done.

Next, you must have Sand tokens in the wallet associated with your Sand profile. Lastly, Ether will be required to cover any transaction costs. If you are keen to buy land during public property sales, go to Sandbox's website and search for the map. You must first select the available land that you wish to buy. The available premium land will be highlighted in yellow, while the standard land will be highlighted in gray.

If you wish to buy the land, simply select the blue buy option. That land would then be reserved until the transaction is finalized. The land would then become purple, signifying that it had already been reserved. Then you will be asked to validate the payment and specify how much gas you have charged and how much ETH you are using.

Once your bank account acknowledges the transaction, the process is complete, and the gas you choose, as well as any blockchain traffic, will have a significant impact on the time it takes to complete the transaction. When your transaction is completed successfully, the land will become red, indicating that you now own it.

Cryptovoxels Land

Cryptovoxels is a blockchain-based virtual reality platform where anybody may build whatever they desire. These structures might be basic dwellings or e-commerce platforms to sell non-fungible tokens (NFTs). It is a motivating destination since cryptocurrency artists worldwide fill the area with amazing stuff. Cryptovoxels quickly transforms into a virtual environment packed with art galleries and a lively community.

Cryptovoxels provides one of the greatest onboarding experiences, claiming to be the simplest and nicest of all. Individuals may sign up for Cryptovoxels, purchase some land, and add virtual things. If they are not creative themselves, they can find artists to help them create a fantastic space

There is a plethora of virtual events to attend. However, one of the difficulties is no centralized mechanism to discover them. You must follow each community separately. Another disadvantage is that you cannot design any advanced games. Aside from those drawbacks, there are several advantages. For example, users can enjoy the same experience on Cryptovoxels whether they use their smartphones or desktop computers.

How to Purchase Cryptovoxel Land

Purchasing land on cryptovoxel is not difficult for individuals who are used to working in the cryptocurrency world, and it is, nevertheless, not cheap. Prices can also change, particularly if additional islands become available. A great plot of land on Cryptovoxels may cost well over $1,000.

Primary sales listings are held every Wednesday at 9 a.m., New Zealand time. If the team has no sales scheduled for the week, they will notify their followers on Twitter or Discord. Users may check the Cryptovoxels page on OpenSea for primary and secondary sales. They can filter the search results by "Recently Created," which is categorized by the following criteria:

Area

Depth

Elevation

Width and Height

Specific Island

Suburbs

Cryptovoxels Auction

It is difficult to acquire at auctions since they usually sell out quickly. In less than ten minutes, 50 items may be delivered. However, it might be interesting to try your luck. If you are interested, here are some suggestions:

- Fill your wallet with ETH (packages are purchased using ETH, not WETH) during the auction. They employ a Dutch auction method, and there is no need to bid or make offers; simply click the purchase button when a price appears).
- Click refresh regularly. The countdown is not particularly exact; it may take a little time for sales to the surface, but property might be gone in seconds once they do.
- Make use of a substantial gas fee. There may be others that click purchase simultaneously as you, and the purchase with the greater gas will win.
- There is not much time to consider the location, size, etc. These sell out quickly! Select the buy option as soon as you locate anything you want at a reasonable price.

Here are some other suggestions:

- Keep an eye on the cryptovoxels Twitter account since changes to the weekly auction schedule occur from time to time. They may also share details about what will be offered and the purchase price.

- You may verify what packages are in the creator's wallet minutes before the countdown timer starts. It does not necessarily imply that they will be put up for sale, but it is possible. You may see bids on some of them; this does not guarantee that they will be accepted, but it is possible. (Yes, this suggestion is a little hazy, but it may be useful.)

Somnium Space Land

Somnium Space is a social and durable virtual reality universe created solely by gamers, with a blockchain-based economy and ownership. You can buy land, create and import items, and monetize your virtual assets immediately. This virtual reality environment is viewable on all major virtual reality headsets and may be visited for free via your web browser. This program competes with many others, like Roblox and Meta, to build the metaverse.

Somnium Space provides users with several options, including:

- Users can invest in the environment by purchasing pieces of land.
- Whatever you build, develop, or showcase has the potential to raise the value of a property.
- With cheap overhead expenses, artists may exhibit their work (like paintings, animations, design, and so on) for everybody to see.
- There is enormous potential for digital office space, training sites, games, and, obviously, monetization in the same way that a real-life firm would.

Land Prices and Availability in Somnium Space

The Somnium Space map features 5,026 land pieces. The price of a plot varies depending on its size, characteristics, and accessibility to desirable elements. Expect plot prices to vary from 3 ETH to over 1,000 ETH. Current plot pricing may be seen on the Somnium Space marketplace.

Buying Land in Somnium Space

Somnium Space does not need users to purchase land to explore the metaverse. Nevertheless, if you want to develop, build, or invest in the environment, you must first learn to buy land. The Somnium Space marketplace allows you to buy and sell land. Every land parcel is a non-fungible token (NFT), which means it is one-of-a-kind and cannot be copied. All land parcels in Somnium Space are kept on the Ethereum blockchain, providing you with complete ownership and control.

Steps to Buy Land in Somnium Space

- **Get a web3 wallet, such as Metamask**

MetaMask is accessed via a browser extension or a smartphone app available on Google Play and the iOS App Store. If you are just starting up, you will have to transfer ETH from Coinbase to your account. Make sure to perform this before selecting a plot of land, as it may take a few days to transfer ETH to your wallet.

- **Locate Land Parcels Using a Web Map**

The good thing about Somnium Space is that you can get a sneak peek of any item without having to sign up with or download any software. The online map's user interface is pretty simple and contains some valuable information, such as:

Height of the parcel

Last price and sale price

You can refer to the recently listed property.

A parcel price heat map.

Once you click on a parcel, a link to the listing on OpenSea is displayed. By entering as a guest or signing in, you may view one land area at a time on the web browser. Go to the main page, get the VR client, and follow the instructions to view the entire environment.

- **Purchase a Plot of Land in the Somnium Space Marketplace**

You will be taken to a web page with the listing after you have clicked on the Somnium Space Marketplace link for any given property. Depending on how the land is advertised, you can instantly acquire land at auction. When you click on a property, you can compare the qualities of the property to other properties on the map. The most recent highest offer is displayed, and also a price history (if there is any sales history)

General Guide to Purchasing Land in the Metaverse

Buying and selling metaverse NFT land is a rather straightforward process that you can readily follow with our help. Purchasing NFT land is the same as purchasing any other NFT item. To begin, all you require is a wallet and some crypto. Before making any buy decisions, like with any business, conduct your research.

- **Decide on a Metaverse Platform**

You must first choose a metaverse platform before purchasing metaverse land. Your objectives for purchasing the land will impact the project you choose. For this section, we will utilize The Sandbox on Ethereum for illustration. However, Decentraland is another popular choice.

- **Prepare your wallet**

You must set up a wallet to access the coins you hold. Depending on your preferences, you can utilize a mobile or browser-supported wallet. Although, using a browser-supported wallet is more likely to result in fewer issues.

Both MetaMask and Binance Chain Wallet are good solutions because they support various blockchains, but make sure the wallet you pick supports the NFT land blockchain. When you first activate your wallet, you will be given a set of words referred to as seed phrases. Keep it somewhere secure since this is how you will be able to reclaim your wallet if you forget it. It is preferable to keep it somewhere that is always offline.

- **Link the wallet to the Sandbox**

You can see tracts of land up for bidding on The Sandbox's page. Many are available directly via The Sandbox marketplace, while others are offered on third-party exchanges such as OpenSea. To keep things simple, we will be considering one we can bid on through The SandBox.

You must first link your wallet before you can bid on anything. Click 'Sign in' in the top right corner of The Sandbox map. Check that the wallet is configured to the same blockchain as the project, in our example, Ethereum.

Then, choose 'MetaMask' A pop-up window will appear inviting you to join to MetaMask. Click the 'Next' button. To continue linking your wallet, select the 'Connect' option. The Sandbox will prompt you to enter your email address and choose a nickname. To complete your account, select 'Continue.' You may also freely supply a password if you want to utilize the SandBox editor.

Select 'Sign' on the MetaMask signature request to ready your account. Once linked, you will see your account balance and personal photo in the upper right corner of the page.

- **Buy SAND or ETH on the Binance platform**

You will need SAND or Ether to buy or bid on the land in your wallet. Purchasing ETH will most certainly be more beneficial since most of The Sandbox land sales accept only ETH. Using your Binance account, you can buy SAND or ETH through a credit or debit card. You will have to move your cryptocurrency to your crypto wallet once you have acquired it. Make a copy of your crypto wallet public address as your withdrawal address.

- **Choose a Piece of LAND**

Using the options available on the page, you can simply search over available land to bid on or acquire in The Sandbox. The majority of The Sandbox land has already been acquired, and therefore, you will generally only find land available on OpenSea. You may, nevertheless, still bid on these sales using The Sandbox map. Because OpenSea connections are included in the UI, the SandBox map is also the best method to ensure that you purchased a legal NFT plot.

When you locate any land you wish to purchase, you can either put an offer by selecting the 'Bid' option or buy it for a set price by selecting the ETH amount. Let us look at placing a bid by selecting 'Bid.' You will then see a pop-up window where you may make an offer. Before finalizing the payment with your wallet, enter the bid amount and select 'Place Bid.' If the seller declines your bid or cancels the auction, the cryptocurrency will be restored to your wallet.

When you select the fixed price, you will be sent to OpenSea to finalize the purchase. Before buying the land, you must first link your wallet to the marketplace. If you do not wish to use The Sandbox, you may offer it via OpenSea.

Selling Land on the Metaverse

When selling your NFT Land, you typically have two alternatives. You can sell it through the metaverse project's marketplace or a secondary marketplace. Only the secondary marketplaces may presently be used for sales on Sandbox, and Landholders will be able to sell directly through The Sandbox in the future for a 5% transaction fee in SAND.

Simply go to your profile and select the 'Sell' option on your NFT to sell your land on OpenSea. After that, you will be able to create a fixed-price or timed auction.

3

LAWS AND PATENT
IN THE METAVERSE

Most of the legal cases that have arisen (or may develop) in the metaverse are intellectual property rights issues that are not specific to the metaverse, but many have a distinctive twist due to the sector's unknown legal territory. Issues about ownership of the underlying intellectual property will be regular and contentious, with billions of dollars at stake. A synopsis of the many theories that will be argued is provided below.

Patents

Under US patent law, the first individual to file for and get a patent for a unique, non-obvious creation enjoys a twenty-year monopoly on that innovation. In contrast to copyright law, whether the subsequent infringing idea was separately produced makes no difference. There will be constant disputes about whether certain technologies violate a metaverse patent, especially given how quickly the metaverse space grows. It will be impossible to distinguish between a "new" innovation and a mere tweak of an existing one.

Contract

A crucial battleground in the contract domain will be who owns metaverse rights under current contracts made before the metaverse was ever considered. This will be akin to fights about who controls VOD rights under contracts established before such rights existed. For instance, if a studio licenses video game rights to a gaming corporation, the gaming corporation may claim ownership of metaverse rights depending on how the deal is written. In the future, it will be important to design contracts with scalpel-like accuracy to ascertain who owns what metaverse rights.

Copyright

Disputes linked to metaverse content are another set of legal concerns. What kinds of things may and cannot be incorporated in metaverse content? The vast majority of cases will come under three categories: copyright, trademark, and right of publicity.

The Copyright Act protects the creator of an original work against third-party duplication. Specifically, there is protection known as "fair use" that, in principle, protects some reproduction based on evaluating some factors specified in the statute. However, in practice, it all boils down to what a judge or jury believes is "fair," so having to depend on fair use protection typically offers little comfort. Notably, in any metaverse that includes cityscapes, the landowners of the property in the metaverse cannot claim copyright for the usage.

If a specific user enters illegally copyrighted content into the metaverse environment, only that user should be found responsible for the violation and not the metaverse corporation. Because the corporation should be shielded by the Digital Millennium Copyright Act (DMCA) safe-harbor provisions, third parties could use DMCA takedown notice protections to withdraw the copyrighted content.

Trademark

Trademark law protects against illegal usage of trademark in a way that leads a participant to assume that the trademark holder was the source of the items or approved or promoted such items. What if the metaverse allows you to drive a Ferrari or wear a Bijan outfit, as is almost certain to happen? Will you believe Ferrari or Bijan invented the metaverse (unlikely) or sponsored it (possibly)? This is a far cry from seeing a Ferrari driving across the screen in a movie, and while some companies have sued for such use in movies, they have always failed. This is because the public believes Ferrari did not make or sponsor the movie. Suppose the metaverse enables participants to interact with the item. If the user must pay digital or real currency to utilize that item, the brands should get much more popularity. In that situation, the conclusion should be no different from selling a toy Ferraris, which needs a Ferrari license.

Claim Against Metaverse Companies

Users will file numerous lawsuits against metaverse corporations, notably for personal harm. The metaverse necessitates using a headset, which prevents the user from seeing the actual world they are in. If they try to wander around at home, they may stumble and tumble down the stairs or through a window. The metaverse can become so realistic and terrifying that 30% of users could not make it across a room with a virtual tightrope walk between the two buildings, resulting in a few heart attacks. The metaverse can produce severe discomfort, even vomiting, when the pictures do not match physical movements. Many individuals may get obsessed with the metaverse, while others may be frightened by its experiences. Without a doubt, there will be lawsuits for negligence and product responsibility filed against metaverse corporations as well as the providers of any device and content.

Claim by User Against User

The most interesting category will be claims by users against other users for various malicious actions committed in the metaverse. Every conceivable crime and tort that may be done in the actual world can also be perpetrated in the metaverse, especially when numerous individuals are involved. There have already been recorded examples of virtual product theft for virtual or real currency and sexual assault by one avatar, which resulted in significant emotional distress to the individual playing the assaulted avatar. What if an avatar raped another and a participant had post-traumatic stress disorder consequently? What if it was a serial offender, and the metaverse company knew it? Such issues are not far away in our unfolding and promising metaverse world.

Current Patent Acquisition

Disney, the multinational entertainment conglomerate, has revealed the acceptance of a patent for metaverse functionality in its theme parks. The firm will employ technology that monitors the activity of Disney park guests' phones. It will then create individualized engaging attractions for each of these guests, shown as 3D graphics on the neighboring physical world, walls, and other park items.

On December 28, 2021, the patent for a 'virtual world simulator in a real place' was authorized. Other metaverse firms describe the technology as web-supported and need virtual reality (VR) or augmented reality (AR) devices. This is not the case with Disney's plan to bring virtual experiences to life. Furthermore, during interactive sessions, this technology will not necessitate the use of headgear.

Nike made its first move into the metaverse. The Oregon-based firm filed numerous additional trademarks indicating its intention to create and sell virtual Nike-branded footwear and clothing.

Nike submitted trademark applications on Oct. 27 for "Nike," the brand's renowned tagline "Just Do It," and the swoosh design. Nike has filed trademarks for 'virtual products' to brand NFTs and video games. Nike is safeguarding their trademarks in this new epoch. People familiar with the company's strategy said the space is a top focus for the company and that customers should expect additional virtual rollouts in the coming months.

4

LUXURY BRANDS AS NFTS
IN THE METAVERSE

High fashion is getting more rooted in the metaverse as the physical and virtual spaces continue to converge. Some believe the metaverse will provide a $50 billion-plus potential for the luxury fashion business over the next decade. Luxury fashion designers are capitalizing on the technological revolution of the metaverse by designing digital clothing specifically for our virtual identities. The metaverse also opens new avenues for businesses to interact with a younger population, as Generation Z is the major group powering and defining digital fashion.

Here are five luxury fashion firms' collaborations that have embraced the metaverse:

Epic Games x Balenciaga

Balenciaga revealed its collaboration with Epic Games, the famous digital game Fortnite. The game has 400 million participants worldwide and has made over $5 billion in sales. The firm created four digital wears and different items for Fortnite avatars, which gamers can buy in-game. Balenciaga and Fortnite physical products were also offered at the brand's shop and website.

Balenciaga has also established its independent business section focused entirely on the metaverse and potentially profitable opportunities. The usefulness of digital clothing is the part that is lacking, but it is making tremendous advances every day. Whether it is unique virtual pets, fashion avatars, or beautifully created virtual environments - developing, trading, owning, and consuming virtual products is the norm for Gen Z.

Fashion firms have so much opportunity to reshape life a decade ahead. This group will be their target market.

Roblox x Gucci

Gucci Garden was launched in May 2021 in collaboration with the metaverse and game platform Roblox. The digital experience was inspired by a real-life exhibition on display in Florence to commemorate the company's 100th anniversary.

The Roblox Gucci Garden, like the original show, had many immersive designed chambers that paid homage to various Gucci ads. Players entered the game in a virtual lobby, where their avatars could explore, try on, and buy virtual Gucci products to wear in the game. Fashion brands must go where no one else is going. The ultimate goal of a fashion brand is to be unique.

No one appreciates the ordinary. An avatar putting on a Gucci belt is unique and possibly even more appealing to a specific audience than finding an actual Gucci bag in a store. The metaverse is new ground, and fashion has become more than a store along the street in a metropolis. We are at a time when the world wants to transcend beyond the industrialized revolution but is unsure how to accomplish it. It is a significant opportunity to expedite improvements, particularly at this pandemic stage.

Roblox x Ralph Lauren

Ralph Lauren has also explored the metaverse, producing The Ralph Lauren Winter Escape in collaboration with Roblox. The game includes a unique gender-neutral virtual fashion set of eight winter sporting outfits. Polo Stores inside the game enable gamers to try on and purchase clothes to customize their avatars. Their involvement in the metaverse is a logical extension of their lifestyle brand. The collaboration with Roblox draws on years of technological innovation and underscores the confidence in the promise that virtual environments and economies bring — particularly for the next generation of customers."

Tencent Games x Burberry

Burberry partnered with Tencent Games in 2020 to create designs for the famous Chinese digital war game Honor of Kings. They developed a character Yao's outfits, known as skins. Burberry's classic trench coat and tartan-patterned ear were included on the skins. By allowing Chinese customers to discover digital items via digital games, they can interact with their communities in a way that truly resonates with them. They intended to encourage their members to explore their environment, whether online or in person.

Barbie x Balmain

In January 2021, Balmain and Barbie unveiled a new collaboration that includes a fully designed clothing and accessories range and three non-fungible tokens (NFTs). MintNFT will sell three distinct Barbie avatars online, each clothed in clothing from the set. The winning bidder will get full possession of the avatar and a unique real-life Barbie-scaled replica of the doll.

Louis Vuitton

In 2021, the French fashion label Louis Vuitton (LV) released a mobile game named LOUIS THE GAME to commemorate its owner's 200th birth anniversary. This is not your typical smartphone game. The game, which includes 30 NFTs, follows the history of the fashion house's mascot Vivienne.

The art collage, created in conjunction with NFT artist Beeple, was valued at USD 69.3 million. However, the NFTs utilized are solely part of the game's collection and are not for sale to the general public. This is not the first LV game that has been created. The fashion label made its gaming breakthrough in 2019 with the release of Endless Runner. The game was inspired by Virgil Abloh's FW19 Runway design and featured retro 16-bit style gameplay.

Nike x RTFKT

Nike x RTFKT is a collaboration between two fashion brands and a non-profit organization. Sneaker fans may try on the new Nike items, but they cannot be worn in public. On December 14, 2021, the shoe behemoth entered the virtual NFT market by acquiring the digital sneaker company RTKFT.

RTKFT held a Snapchat digital "try on" session for the sneakers, after which buyers could join the virtual auction. The winners received physical shoes, but digital shoes remain the most sought-after asset. Since RTKFT studios announced their affiliation with Nike Inc., its popularity has skyrocketed. Most of their digital footwear have striking similarities and are inspired by Nike signatures such as Air Jordan 1 and Air Force 1.

This acquisition is another move that facilitates Nike's technological change and enables them to serve athletes and designers at the crossroads of sports, creative thinking, gaming and culture. They're accumulating a skilled team of designers with a genuine and connected brand. They plan to invest in the RTFKT brand, serve and develop their creative and innovative society and broaden Nike's virtual footprint and prowess.

Overpriced

Consider buying a hoodie that can be scanned to show your own NFTs, that too on the go. Yes, this is no more a futuristic idea to be actualized. Fashion brand Overpriced has announced a set of such NFT hoodies, carrying codes exclusive to the owner.

If misplaced, the buyer is given a new code, and the previous code will no longer be used for selling. Ten smart hoodies were auctioned for USD 26,000 during the NFT market platform Block Party's first auction on 13 April 2021, while the rest 25 were given to entertainment and fashion industry stars.

How Companies Can Explore the Metaverse

The metaverse space will play an increasingly important role in effective brand strategies. Businesses will have new opportunities to enhance brand loyalty and interact with their (future) customers creatively by giving a unique experience with the emergence of an immersive environment. The two businesses listed below use unique and very creative methods to engage with their customers. These businesses demonstrate how sales promotion can be interesting and entertaining by being the first to the metaverse.

Wendy's - Keeping Fortnite Fresh

In 2018, Fortnite included a new event called Food Fight, which allowed gamers to represent their favorite virtual restaurant, Durr Burger (Team Burger) or Pizza Pit (Team Pizza). The last man standing was proclaimed the winner. Wendy's opted to play the game to make their advertising more entertaining to the viewers. They noticed that the Durr Burger burgers were kept in the refrigerator, against Wendy's known policy of never using frozen beef.

Wendy's recognized a new chance to promote their "fresh, never frozen beef." They went on Twitch, made a figure that looked like the brand's mascot, dropped it into Fortnite, and began destroying all the refrigerators in the game's Food Fight mode rather than killing other gamers. Wendy's mission was live-streamed on Twitch, asking hundreds of thousands of people to watch and help them demolish refrigerators rather than murdering other gamers. Over nine hours of broadcasting, 1.5 million minutes were viewed on Twitch, and brand mentions increased by 119% across social media. Wendy's decision paid off, with the company receiving multiple prizes, including eight Cannes Lions.

Coca-Cola – NFT Auction

Coca-Cola introduced a non-fungible token (NFT) collection in July 2021, which sold for $575,000 in an online auction. The firm used the influence of its name to propel its collection and earn more than $50,000 for charity in 72 hours. Going into the NFT and metaverse space will give customers "the same iconic and positive experiences they are acquainted with in real life in the virtual environment.

On International Friendship Day, Coca-Cola sold four multi-sensory, friendship-inspired non-fungible tokens through the OpenSea exchange. It was sold off as a single loot box, a pun on the famous video game element of sealed mystery boxes. Not only did the winner get these four non-fungible tokens, but they also got a fridge loaded with Coca-Cola drinks and other goodies. The NFT auction created a lot of interest in the cryptocurrency world and depicted Coca-Cola as a forward-thinking firm that recognizes exactly where its customers are.

5

METAVERSE STOCKS

All business recently appears to have ambitious plans for the metaverse. Some firms are beginning small by selling non-fungible tokens (NFTs) in exchange for virtual products, while others want to develop complete virtual worlds. With so much promising news and collaborations in the space, it is wise to consider what businesses are leading the race and are good for investment. So, we will look at some firms that might benefit from this long-term trend and permanently alter how we connect.

Meta-Platforms

The Meta Platforms firm, previously known as Facebook, changed its name to reflect its future ambitions in the metaverse. Many of the basic components for such a virtual environment are already in place.

Every month, 3.58 billion individuals use at least one of its products (Facebook, Messenger, Instagram, or WhatsApp). Over the last year, it has sold over 10 million Quest 2 virtual reality headsets, and it has now unveiled Horizon Worlds. This virtual reality environment will allow those headset users to connect. It just unveiled its first set of smart glasses and intends to offer more advanced augmented reality headsets in the future.

As Meta assembles all those elements, it will extend its scope well beyond computers and smartphones. People will soon be seeing one other's profiles in the virtual world or scanning real-world objects with AR technologies. In other words, it has the potential to turn the entire planet into a massive computer platform. Hence it has the potential to pull tremendous traffic, which in turn presents a profitable opportunity for an investor

Roblox

Roblox's aims are not as ambitious as Meta's, but they are more straightforward. The Roblox platform allows users to create basic block-supported worlds and games for one another without any coding experience. It is extremely popular among youngsters, and its designers may monetize their games by using in-game money called Robux.

Since it depends on its community of roughly 50 million daily active users to develop and explore new virtual spaces, Roblox is a self-sufficient environment. The growth of that environment will persuade more businesses to create their worlds within Roblox's world to reach more customers. That is why Nike has just created Nikeland, a virtual theme park on Roblox that allows gamers to partake in virtual sports events. These metaverse-based promotions might overtake conventional marketing mechanisms if additional companies follow Nike's lead.

Nintendo

Nintendo has many of the components required to build a vast metaverse environment. Since March 2017, it has delivered 98.1 million Switches, hybrid devices that quickly swapped between home console and portable modes. Carrying a Switch is less burdensome than wearing virtual reality headgear, and the devices can easily be transformed into VR headgear using a Labo kit. Because of its adaptability, the Switch is an excellent platform for launching immersive multiplayer games like Animal Crossing: New Horizons.

Nintendo has already sold roughly 35 million copies of animal crossing worldwide. The blockbuster game is already a mini-metaverse that lets users own houses, undertake tasks to earn in-game cash, and communicate with other players. Hence, the stock demonstrates a profitable opportunity to look out for.

Match Group

Match Group, the online dating behemoth that runs Tinder and a slew of other popular dating platforms, has over 16 million paying customers globally. Match's dating platforms, on their own, might be regarded as metaverse products that enable individuals to meet one other online.

On the other hand, Match has considerably bigger ambitions for the metaverse. Single Town, a new feature, is now being tested on college campuses in Seoul, South Korea. The program allows users to converse via virtual avatars in virtual spaces such as a bar or a park, and it is similar to a dating-oriented Animal Crossing. The Match Group already sees "encouraging early signals" regarding engagement rates among Gen Z users on Single Town, implying similar game-like elements for its other dating platforms are on the way.

Unity

It is difficult to create immersive 3D content. Creators require graphics, lighting, and physics technologies and a robust engine capable of rendering content rapidly. Developers were typically forced to design those tools in-house, which meant they had to invest many resources in a project before providing any content. Even then, the content had to be recoded for each platform separately. Unity eliminates this complication.

Unity software enables developers to create and execute immersive 2D and 3D visual experiences that can be distributed over more than 20 systems, including iOS, Android, and Windows, without the need for recoding. Unity also provides features for in-app marketing, in-app sales, and user analytics, which aid in the monetization of developers' content.

Unsurprisingly, the scope of Unity's portfolio has resulted in high demand in the gaming industry. Unity is used by 94 of the top 100 game production teams. However, its platform is also being used in other areas. Architects, for example, use Unity to design building projects, while retailers use it to generate digital marketing materials. This shows the potential surrounding Unity stock.

Unity's firm is doing well financially. Unity earned $34 million in positive free cash flow in the third quarter of 2021 and has a debt-free financial statement with $1.3 billion in cash and short-term assets. In the future, Unity's development engine is projected to play a crucial part in creating the metaverse. Whether virtual environments or several, the metaverse will be packed with immersive, real-time 3D material that responds quickly to participant inputs. In other words, kicking a rock in the metaverse causes it to roll over the virtual ground. And Unity's technology enables this. It is now the top content creation engine for AR and VR applications.

The firm now estimates its market potential to be $29 billion, but it expects to increase as technologies such as the metaverse evolve. In summary, Unity has a solid competitive position and a developing market potential. As a result, this stock has the potential to deliver massive gains to owners.

Nvidia

The metaverse is entirely online and requires PC hardware to function. Knowing this, is there a better metaverse stock for investment than Nvidia? The firm is well-known for its graphics processing units (GPUs), operating in other markets. GPUs were designed to produce 3D graphics but have since found various applications. Because of its capacity to conduct computations fast, GPUs now drive gaming systems, engineering simulations, and storage systems.

Nvidia has evolved into more than simply a hardware firm; it is now a software supplier. Its Omniverse solution is the most significant metaverse software. It allows for easier interaction on 3D projects and replicates each design to provide the most realistic picture. Nvidia's Omniverse Avatar, for instance, integrates "voice AI, computer vision, natural language understanding, recommendation engines, and simulation technologies" to produce real virtual assistants who can help with tasks such as customer service or restaurant orders. Nvidia will continue to innovate to assure the strength of its metaverse solutions.

Even though Nvidia earned more than $7 billion in sales in the third quarter of 2021 alone, it is expanding at a 50% annual rate. Its operational expenditures increased by just 25%, resulting in an 84 percent rise in earnings. Nvidia has various business categories, all of which are active.

Professional visualization, or metaverse creation, is rapidly rising but accounts for just 8% of total income, whereas gaming and data centers account for 45 and 41%, respectively. Expectedly, the professional visualization income share will expand if the metaverse becomes more generally accepted. Hardware vendors used to have a cyclical reputation since demand fluctuated with the innovation cycle. Most items, from vehicles to workstations, already have a GPU, and Nvidia is continuously delivering new models, shortening the cycle to the point that it is no longer cyclical. Moreover, its software goods do not go through the same cyclical nature as hardware. Consequently, during the last decade, its price-to-earnings ratio has increased. Given how fast Nvidia is extending its use cases, it is a wonderful investment irrespective of how successful the metaverse develops.

Matterport

Matterport is yet another intriguing metaverse project. This organization digitizes tangible assets. The digitized asset can subsequently be utilized for design, operations, or other visualization types. Typical sectors that profit includes real estate, retail, hospitality, and construction. The firm has 439,000 users and annual revenue of $111 million. The stock peaked at more than $37.00 in late 2021, but it currently trades at a 58 percent discount to that high.

Apple

Apple is another organization looking to the metaverse to improve its already excellent results. According to rumors, the organization will release its augmented and virtual reality headset in 2022, with a lighter, better version to follow in 2024. Given the organization's 1 billion iPhone users as its primary client base, the opportunity here is enormous. All investors should be vying here.

The prospect of a new revenue source to complement the iPhone, Mac, and iPad has investors drooling, temporarily pushing the company's price beyond $3 trillion. Apple's fiscal 2021 results were outstanding. Revenues increased by 33% to $365.8 billion, while operating income increased by 64% to $108.9 billion. Similarly, diluted EPS increased by 71% to $5.61. Because of the company's aggressive share buyback plan, EPS climbed faster than operating income. The buybacks are favorable since they reduce its outstanding shares, raising EPS more quickly. They are also a tax-deferred capital return to investors.

Due to market forecasts for the future year and the new product introduction, Apple's current forward P/E ratio of 30 is higher than historical norms. Some believe it is overpriced; yet, do not gamble against this stock or this firm.

Walmart

Is Walmart a metaverse investment? Yes, in a way. CNBC reported in January 2022 that the massive retailer is planning to join the metaverse. In December 2021, Walmart filed additional trademarks relating to selling digital items and supplying virtual currency and NFTs. Maybe it is a little early to categorize Walmart as a metaverse stock. In a statement to CNBC and other media sites, the firm stated that it is constantly examining how new technology may affect the future retail experience.

Nevertheless, if the metaverse reaches its full potential, Walmart may find a huge potential in it. Walmart's stock is also considerably more fairly priced than most stocks of organizations with metaverse ambitions. Its stock is now trading at 20.4 times projected profits.

Electronics Arts Inc.

The next on the list is Electronic Arts, a video game firm that is also one of the world's leading gaming companies. The company is still leading the way in changing the way consumers play video games. It is a global leader in immersive digital entertainment, creating games for web-connected consoles, smartphones, and PCs. EA stock is now trading at $132.63 as of 1:02 p.m. ET.

What is the organization's financial situation? According to the organization's quarterly report, aggregate revenue in the final quarter of 2021 was $1.82 billion, up 58.6 percent year on year. The net revenue for the quarter was $294 million, or $1.02 per share diluted. It also paid a cash dividend of $0.17 per share during the quarter.

Amazon Inc.

Amazon is yet another name to focus on among tech behemoths that might gain from the metaverse. The majority of this would be due to Amazon Web Services (AWS), the industry's top cloud computing provider. In principle, firms from different sectors might use AWS's on-demand cloud computing capabilities. The likes would serve as a significant basis for forthcoming participants creating their own metaverse experiences. As of 1:03 p.m. ET, AMZN stock is trading at $3,313.29 per share. Despite Amazon's main departments' overall progress, analysts appear to predict the additional potential for AMZN stock. Some people have offered bullish updates on the company's stock.

Many highlight Amazon's strong future growth potential as an important driver for these changes. Between 2023 and 2025, the corporation is expected to go through a major infrastructure investment cycle. Is AMZN stock your top selection among metaverse stocks due to all of this?

Advanced Micro Devices Inc.

Advanced Micro Devices (AMD) is a global semiconductor business that creates PCs chips and similar technologies. With over 50 years of industry expertise, the business is still driving new development, particularly in high-performance computing, graphics, and visualization systems. Its products and services are utilized by many other organizations worldwide. AMD stock is presently trading at $138.25 as of 1:01 p.m. ET, up more than 40% in the year 2021.

Gather

Gather is a network for video chat. Gather bridges the gap between people and suggests innovative ways to engage with new people to develop a virtual community. It develops a metaverse platform for virtual workplaces, conferences, and gatherings. It involves creating a virtual layer on top of the earth's physical layer where people may communicate, mingle, and have fun. The virtual reality environment will provide a spice of pleasure to an otherwise mundane life.

Gather's virtual reality platform is unique in that it can give a virtual experience without the need for a virtual reality headset. Gather is currently developing a metaverse world that is open to anyone and will give individuals a break from their busy daily life. Pixel graphics will be used in the Gather virtual reality environments to spice up the platform's uniqueness. Murder mystery games are also played in gathering contexts. Later on, the platform will host different games in virtual reality worlds. This makes the company a prospect in the metaverse.

Tencent

Tencent is a Chinese multinational company that offers virtual products and services to help individuals lead better lives. It was established in 1998, and Tencent now offers e-commerce, mobile commerce, internet, and payment services. Through its game creation business TiMi Studio Group, the multiservice provider, concentrates on the metaverse. Tencent will focus on the metaverse approach, specifically through its game production branch Tencent Games, with many prominent firms in its portfolio.

Roblox and Epic Games will face real competition from Tencent Games. Tencent is confident about metaverse technologies at the moment. It will create a gaming, social networking, search marketing, and open, collaborative network. Users will be able to work with other companies on Tencent's multiverse platform, which will allow them to play, communicate, and relax digitally. It is all set up to put meta in direct competition.

Tinder

Tinder is a dating platform that was first released in 2012. Tinder uses the right swipe to connect like-minded folks on its platform. Tinder has grown into a platform for meeting friends and possible lovers over time. Companies from several domains have entered the metaverse. Tinder is creating a dating metaverse and connecting people through digital avatars. Some new features, such as "Swipe Night" and "Explore," have already been released.

Tinder will also introduce tinder coins to take the plunge with cryptocurrencies. With the dating metaverse on the horizon, Tinder's virtual dating environment is bound to set some high bar. Tinder allows Gen Z to explore and play the virtual interactive game by allowing them to dance along with their virtual avatars and make new friends.

Tinder is now concentrating on building the metaverse platforms from the ground up, with Tinder's virtual economy in place. The world may anticipate terms such as space dating and metaverse dating to become a reality. Tinder's metaverse platform will be where digital avatars may meet real people.

6

METAVERSE BUSINESS
ENTRY, DO'S AND DON'TS

When a company invests in a virtual space and the public declares a moment, it is sensible to take a step back and assess if it can live up to the expectations. However, if this is the "meta" moment —if it provides something that the public truly desires — it makes sense to assume that many businesses ask what the metaverse is and if they should enter the space. Even knowing where to begin might be difficult for companies considering navigating this new area.

A few businesses have already begun to shape the environment, with entertainment and gaming giants leading the way. For organizations that are yet to enter the space, each brand must discover its niche and weigh the risk-reward ratio. Doing so necessitates understanding what is possible, and organizations that are diving in quickly may both inspire and serve as pilot projects. For example, many firms are capitalizing on the metaverse's gaming aspect by offering brand experiences that are effectively virtual and interactive sponsorships.

The commercial use cases of the metaverse are being boosted even further by new behaviors centered on purchasing items and services directly from social interactions, commonly known as "social commerce." Social commerce is becoming a greater portion of US e-commerce over time, with a predicted $36 billion in 2021 alone. As capabilities expand, new business models for investors, virtual products — like non-fungible tokens (NFTs), unique creations sold and protected on a blockchain — and commerce on tangible goods acquired in virtual spaces will all gain prominence.

Brands should always be testing and learning, and the digital world necessitates inquisitive and innovative thinking. The metaverse promise to be the next evolution of how humans use the internet to interact, engage, and trade – staying on the sidelines for too long seems unlikely.

Here are some examples of what businesses can do right now:

Choose Your Targets

Consider how much time your target audiences/users spend in the metaverse and adjust your activities and mode of operation accordingly. Companies concentrating on younger groups, for instance, are unlikely to have the opportunity to sit out the metaverse space for long. Who are your target audiences, and what patterns are trending with your present and future audiences that indicate how quickly you should move into the metaverse?

Watch The Competition

Begin by discussing cases where rival firms do things in the metaverse, such as a presentation at a leadership meeting, to get the discussion across to the executive team. Much of the sector may be daunting, especially when seemingly incomprehensible ideas like NFTs or blockchain are included. Can you appoint someone to advocate for these issues, bringing relatable, practical experiences to every meeting?

Check for Applications

Examine whether the metaverse provides opportunities for your firm to explore different experiences and expedite your objective or future goals, such as sustainability. Almost all businesses have made, or will soon be making, a public commitment to ESGs relating to sustainability. What can you explore in the metaverse to see if you can find more sustainable ways to serve your audiences?

Plan Your Entry

Propose that your agency team start developing an idea on how your company should appear in the metaverse and when it would make sense. Holding businesses and independent agencies are both closely monitoring mass media habits and developing trends, so this is an excellent time to inquire about what they are seeing throughout their client portfolio. What tests might they put in place to allow you to introduce your business to the metaverse safely?

Maintain Your Balance

If you are currently in it, be aware that all new environments provide risk and reward; manage appropriately, recognizing that it may be very uncertain and poor in standards. The good thing is that the current pandemic has made us all far more adaptable than we have ever been. To say the obvious, there will be failures in trials. Second Life gave the allure of the metaverse some years ago, but the risk for the companies that engaged was neither large nor long term. So, if now is the time, it is critical to determine how to be there.

Most importantly, individuals should consider unlocking their creative and narrative abilities in product marketing or leadership positions. If the creative palette grows in the metaverse, we ought to be delighted to design experiences at any stage in the user journey, from acquisition through engagement, purchase, and customer service, that has the promise to be both stunning and sleeker than before. And eventually, we will probably wish to easily transition from actual to virtual environments, which will be the next frontier.

Make Use of Technology

Products that were previously deemed too personal to be sold online have gained appeal thanks to the application of AR and VR. Customers may virtually enter a shop, peruse products, and even try on shoes thanks to the advent of virtual shops on Snapchat, for instance. Leveraging existing technologies while keeping an eye out for emerging breakthroughs enables organizations to capitalize on the potential of current platforms, such as AR and VR while offering an enhanced consumer experience within the metaverse. Ray-Ban is one company that is taking this step, expanding on current AR features that allow users to digitally try on glasses or developing smart eyewear tailored for engagement in the metaverse.

Innovation is increasingly important in today's digital world, where users compare any virtual experience against the top companies. Whatever the size of a company, the virtual experience must equal or surpass the expectations of users who are accustomed to Amazon's speed and service. The same is valid across sectors. A new streaming service, for instance, will fail if it lacks the speed, usability, and offers that a generation of Netflix users has come to appreciate. Big platforms establish high standards for everyone worldwide.

Go Where the Customers Are

Though the metaverse will enable improved experiences through global connectedness, the primary platforms that operate inside it will continue to produce separate interaction pathways. Amazon may build a digital store environment where users could stroll, explore, pick, and purchase things dispatched to their homes. This is similar to how Meta already offers an immersive shopping experience on Instagram, complete with in-app virtual stores, product tags, and checkout choices. Five Guys might develop a digital restaurant where customers could view the menu, chat with a customer service avatar, and order meals via DoorDash or UberEats. The options are limitless.

All of this indicates that users in the metaverse will be more scattered than ever before, yet they will still seek instant satisfaction. The days of driving visitors to an eCommerce site through interaction channels are long gone. Today's modern buyer, regardless of channel, expects to know about a product, tap to buy it, and have it shipped within 24 hours. Brands must change to capitalize on these prospects.

Produce an Endless Number of Assets

Attention is monetized through advertising. With customer interactions spanning every medium possible and on every device available, customer attention is more divided than ever. Marketers must understand all platforms thoroughly and create what appears to be a limitless amount of assets to feed each one effectively. Add to that the consumer expectation of first-rate experiences irrespective of media or network, and creating a compelling digital experience gets considerably more challenging. But it is also important if a company wants to keep up; failing to change quickly may lead to the death of any business, irrespective of earlier success.

Consider any typical household from the user's perspective. At any point in time, family members may be gazing at various devices, engaged in diverse places, and consuming content suited to their preferences and behavior patterns. Businesses that want to be top-of-mind for even five minutes must work harder than ever to be in the right location, provide the appropriate content, and spark the ideal interaction. Every component is equally important. What is the payoff? Those that put in the work will receive the benefits of a more enhanced, engaging consumer experience, as well as the brand loyalty that it may generate.

Businesses will have to spend time and money in channel strategy and create unlimited content to fuel interaction to stay competitive and successfully interact in the metaverse.

7

ROLE OF BLOCKCHAIN
IN THE METAVERSE

Blockchain is a system that records transactions permanently, generally in a decentralized and online system known as a ledger. The most popular blockchain-based cryptocurrency is Bitcoin. When you purchase bitcoin, the transaction is logged to the Bitcoin blockchain network, shared between thousands of separate computers across the world.

This decentralized monitoring system is extremely difficult to manipulate or distort. In comparison to conventional banking systems, online blockchains like Bitcoin and Ethereum are also transparent — all transactions are open to anybody on the network. On a blockchain network, products like artwork and music are non-fungible tokens (NFTs).

What does all of this blockchain cryptocurrency asset madness have to do with the metaverse? Everything! To begin, the blockchain enables the ownership of digital assets in a virtual environment. You will possess that NFT in the physical world and the virtual world.

Furthermore, the metaverse is not being constructed by a single organization or corporation. Separate organizations will create different virtual worlds, eventually interoperable — establishing the metaverse. People will want to bring their belongings with them when they move between virtual environments, like from Decentraland's virtual spaces to Microsoft's. The blockchain will confirm ownership of your virtual products in both virtual environments if two virtual environments are compatible. You can access your cryptocurrency products as long as you can access your cryptocurrency wallet.

The objective of the metaverse is to give individuals a virtual reality experience that, in many respects, may outperform physical reality in terms of experiences and possibilities. Blockchain's unhackability and integrity are crucial features for any virtual reality platform to acquire widespread acceptance. Hacks and privacy violations are routine, but if individuals function online and virtual, the fundamental platform on which they will operate should be protected.

Blockchain enables quick information verification and enables cryptographically safe and secured payments. Blockchain is a critical component of how virtual reality will be deployed. The metaverse will need and expect trades executed on-demand, which blockchain may enable. Transactions are required for a realistic virtual reality world to function and work as promised, and these transfers must be safe and almost instantaneous. Individuals in this environment will have to be able to: a) trade and interact as easily as if they were in reality, and b) be confident that these transactions will be executed.

Blockchain transactions, viable and established technologies, allow people and organizations to make digital, transparent, and real-time transactions. However, even if blockchain technologies are not used permanently, the move toward digital and online payments is expanding. Transacting and partaking in business has become a popular progression, growing even more prevalent with the introduction of cryptocurrency payments by Visa, Mastercard, and PayPal.

Blockchain-based payments become even more common in a virtual environment, like the metaverse. It stands to reason that such transactions will continue to rise to prominence in the future. The metaverse is still a new and quickly growing field. Blockchain will need to play a substantial role in its future application to enable and realize a fully working metaverse.

Blockchain Assures Authenticity

In the metaverse, the blockchain's digital signature process and distributed nature can assist authors in proving that they are the true owners of a certain material, as well as users in proving that they are authentic users. Using blockchain might decrease NFT counterfeits in the metaverse since each node authenticates the status and possession of all assets on the system, preventing them from being reproduced or altered.

It is not only about virtual products. In the future, when individuals upload their memory into the metaverse, we cannot verify that their memories are not changed or manipulated by anybody without the validation and verification provided by the blockchain. Storing metaverse information, data, NFTs, pictures, and other artworks on the blockchain ensure permanent storage since the data becomes permanent.

This will prevent unauthorized tampering with anything of value held in the metaverse. The FIO protocol allows creators to register their work with a readily accessible address that works as a one-of-a-kind signature for their work, prohibiting NFT frauds. However, there are risks. There is the risk of user error. Users mistype large, sophisticated addresses or experience man-in-the-middle assaults, which might lead to millions of dollars being transferred to the incorrect destination or stolen permanently.

Many current metaverses and virtual environments are successful because they gamify social and brand interactions. Blockchain-based metaverse platforms provide stronger digital incentive mechanisms for this gamification. This includes tokens and in-world virtual currency. The metaverse will enable peer-to-peer interactions to provide employment, economic power, lending, and trade. The metaverse and NFTs certification solutions will serve as a virtual business-enabled financial system.

This gamification will expand art, luxury fashion, collectives, history, cities, and real estate in the metaverse. Blockchain provides a platform to trade products and services, such as game incentives and betting in the metaverse. Users in Decentraland, for example, can purchase NFTs with cryptocurrencies or the platform token MANA thanks to the blockchain network.

Blockchain can be utilized to control in-metaverse currencies, and this ensures a robust and open economy by providing us with protection and transaction authentication for our purchases and exchanges. There have even been networks in OpenSim that utilized Bitcoin, like YrGrid in 2015. However, none of these initiatives took off owing to the high maintenance and overhead expenses of using the unpredictable Bitcoin currency for in-world payments.

Blockchain Prospects for the Metaverse

The Blockchain network has struggled to find practical applications outside of ransomware and speculative projects like Bitcoin and NFTs. There have been some pilot projects in many sectors, but they have seldom resulted in substantial business effects because of security, scalability, efficiency, and cost concerns.

Now, cryptocurrency enthusiasts are focusing on the metaverse as a place where the blockchain may have an influence. Proponents of NFT argue that it is a superior means of personalizing art and material in the metaverse. Also, the blockchain networks can decentralize and safeguard metaverse products. Furthermore, there is no governance because the blockchain is based on decentralized storage — each member has a copy of the blockchain.

Blockchain can liberate business by tokenizing physical assets for sale on metaverse platforms. This allows the digital exchange of products that could not previously be electronically exchanged. Digital passports, like those suggested by ARCx, may aid in credit scoring, collateralized lending, and decentralized trade.

Blockchain and Gaming in the Metaverse

Despite the enormous enthusiasm around the notion, the metaverse will remain a collection of ideas. The quantity and types of organizations engaged in virtual worlds outside gaming firms will be the most revealing change in the early phases of development. Nevertheless, even non-gaming organizations will rely on gaming technology and engines to develop the standardized protocols needed for a huge network of interconnected environments.

Businesses, too, may get a head start on the metaverse by focusing on gaming. Rather than pursuing vague and buzzy possibilities still in the "proof of concept" stage, smart businesses will use the opportunity afforded by learning from gaming, which has featured networked virtual environments for almost 50 years.

Given the vast virtual platform that the metaverse provides, digital ownership will be essential, resulting in greater interest in the notion of blockchain. In the short term, blockchain-supported games have proven to be the most promising application. This is more likely to supplement the conventional gaming sector than an upheaval. The popularity of these games, in particular, may parallel the rise of mobile casual games instead of cannibalizing current game users. Blockchain gaming will broaden the scope of gaming to include participants motivated by monetary gain. It will legitimize professional gaming beyond performative components like streaming or competitions.

Big Business

Given the relevance of blockchain networks to the metaverse, there will be huge investment opportunities for business. Klatyn, for instance, is a blockchain choice developed for gaming. Klaytn, developed by internet giant Kakao Corp in 2019, has garnered local popularity via integration with the KakaoTalk chat software. It also serves as the blockchain network for the Central Bank Digital Currency (CBDC) initiative in collaboration with the Bank of Korea via private blockchain deployment.

Klaytn is taking a step toward the metaverse, tailoring the whole platform for metaverse applications. AAA games, play-to-earn (P2E) games, non-fungible tokens (NFTs), and enabling DeFi services for metaverse enterprises are among them. Given the expertise of its 31 Governance Council members in blockchain, social networks, digital products, gaming, and entertainment, Klaytn is set to thrive in this burgeoning field.

Klaytn hopes to create a seamless onboarding process for metaverse designers to simply put their games and online worlds on the network to accomplish this objective. These are some of the projects that will be implemented by Klaytn this year that could provide inspiration:

- The release of a game developer bundle that comprises a collection of Klaytn L2 solutions, a chosen list of open source tools, and a Software Development Kit (SDK)
- In Q2 2022, Ethereum equivalence will be supported, allowing EVM-based dapps to be onboarded without change.
- Community-building strategies to boost individual project user growth.
- Management and financial assistance for initiatives with significant global prospects

Due to the popularity of video games in Korea and the widespread dominance of K-culture, Klaytn aims to be the blockchain network of choice for the gaming industry, particularly AAA titles. There is currently no other blockchain network that is properly tailored for the metaverse, with immense job opportunities and a creative economy. Hence, your objective can be big but certainly attainable.

In 2021, the blockchain network had a breakthrough year, with Bitcoin reaching a new record high of $68,789. Nonfungible tokens, meme tokens, and the expansion of the decentralized financial sector captivated the public's attention. With 2021 behind us, 2022 is already setting itself a year of continued development and expansion. The industry leader ICICB group is preparing to revolutionize the industry by introducing the world's quickest blockchain, intended to overcome the present restrictions faced by the top networks.

The idea was first announced at the 2021 Blockchain Innovation Summit in Dubai. It came to completion when the ICICB group collaborated with the world-famous video game manufacturer Atari to develop the Atari Chain and Atari token. As newbies enjoy the platform's ease of use, it is emerging as a new wave of popularity for blockchain networks and cryptos. The platform contains a suite of tools to make the blockchain experience easier for creators and consumers.

During the last several years, the ICICB Group's objective has been to create and grow digital technology, which has been incorporated into everyday life to promote efficiency and sustainability. The group is now focusing on the burgeoning subject of the blockchain network. It aims to redefine user involvement and facilitate integration with all areas of society, such as decentralized payments, entertainment, investment, and engineering.

The ICICB Group was the primary sponsor of the Blockchain Innovation Summit, which gathered up industry experts in networking, entrepreneurship, and innovation to raise awareness of blockchain technology, smart contracts, and their possibilities, as well as the quickly expanding metaverse.

ICICB is pushing things to the next level with its new blockchain platform. This is only the beginning of its goals, which also involve the establishment of a fully operational, blockchain-supported casino and a metaverse platform. Both will work with the platform's own decentralized crypto wallet and mobile apps.

The Luxury, a project that will turn the IT sector into a decentralized virtual-reality platform and redesign the whole user experience using augmented reality and blockchain, has received a $10 million investment from the organization.

ICICB Group is committed to using its significant knowledge to serve its worldwide customer network of 114 investment branch locations in 26 countries. To provide the most excellent user-facing blockchain network, the organization is dedicated to servicing many industries, including health care, manufacturing, water, education, and tourism. This presents a huge opportunity and possibilities for brands and creators to pioneer technology and products in the metaverse.

Blockchain Projects in the Metaverse

Below are a few blockchain projects that will be included in metaverse environments as they develop.

Ethereum D'Apps

The Ethereum blockchain was the first to be powered by smart contracts. Vitalik Buterin and his colleagues coined many of the phrases still used in the industry today. Ethereum developed the decentralized application (D'App) ecosystem with its various standards. Hence, the Ethereum Virtual Machine (EVM) has become a web3 space standard. Many blockchains are EVM compatible and have additional capabilities.

These constraints have not stopped developers from running metaverse projects on the Ethereum network. Radio Caca (CACA), Star Atlas (ATLAS), Game Credits (Game), RedFox Labs (RFOX), and others are among these projects. As the journey toward ETH2.0 progresses, we will also notice a significant movement toward the metaverse. For years to come, ETH2.0 will be an environment that defines norms inside the web 3.0 tempo.

Telos

Telos' blockchain network is one of such platforms that allow developers to thrive in a safe environment. Telos is becoming a center for metaverse communities and their related uses because of its dual-purpose EVM and EOS features. Cards&Tokens, Kolobook, Koin, APPICS, and other Telos metaverse apps are examples.

As the Telos blockchain network continues to expand and evolve, we will see a rise in developers that wish to move their applications to multi-tier blockchains and ledgers. Telos has been at the center of developing technologies that will continue to make headlines in the metaverse and beyond.

Avalanche

Avalanche, which will be introduced in the middle of 2020, is one of the most promising web3 blockchains. Once onboard, the Avalanche system provides several benefits to developers. The Avalanche blockchain's acceleration, development, and venture capital mechanisms have drawn metaverse developers to the network. Kalao, ApeIn, and Kryptomon are among them.

Avalanche has several characteristics that make it ideal for metaverse applications. Because of the availability of three subchains, X-Chain, C-Chain, and P-Chain, developers may design projects with a wide range of features and needs. Its rapid transaction rates ensure scalability, while Proof-of-Stake assures that transaction costs remain among the lowest in the crypto market.

Qtum Blockchain

Qtum, a rising blockchain, has enormous promise. Its Proof-of-Stake (PoS) UTXO paradigm highlights this potential, enabling smart contract execution and scalability. Qtum's most recent halving event has recently concluded. The increasing token scarcity will have an impact on QTUM token demand.

Smart Contract, Blockchain, and the Metaverse

Smart contracts are essentially programs that run when certain criteria are satisfied and are recorded on a blockchain. They are often used to automate a deal so that all parties are confident of the outcome. They can also automate a process by initiating the next operation when certain circumstances are satisfied.

The introduction of blockchains supported by smart contracts has resulted in new paradigms for metaverse technology. Smart contracts establish a model in which decentralized apps exist in metaverse environments and multiple blockchains. Many features may be included in smart contract criteria. Within a metaverse architecture, these qualities enable higher engagement and use-case situations.

Need for Smart Contract in the Metaverse

Smart contracts are the propeller that drives all of the activities in blockchain networks. Blockchain feature is coded for every decentralized app. Due to the features blockchains provide, smart contracts for metaverses perform extremely due to their decentralized nature.

Blockchains aid in the security of metaverse activity. They are appropriate for trade and all forms of internet business. Blockchains also aid in connecting metaverse participants who are not required to be localized. Issues like internet connection and insufficient capacity pose challenges for centralized systems. Smart contracts on blockchains allow for interactions inside metaverse networks while also allowing for transaction redundancy. They enable more innovation without increasing the expense factor found in centralized technology.

Working smart contracts offer very little or no maintenance expenses, and it enables faster development and cheaper operating expenses for project developers. Finally, smart contracts allow new features to the metaverses without modifying the metaverse framework. As metaverse environments become more prevalent in our daily lives, we will see smart contracts, D'apps, and use-cases emerge.

8

NFTS IN THE METAVERSE

S ince the recent madness with metaverse space, there has been a huge surge in enthusiasm and investment in NFTs, which are truly the metaverse's fiber. NFTs are what will allow you to own real estate in the metaverse. They let you own virtual products and so on, and they are now skyrocketing.

Will the NFT Market Explode in Metaverse

There has been a significant increase in NFT sales. According to statistics supplied by DappRadar, the overall value of all NFT transactions in 2021 was $23 billion. According to many sources, the NFT area witnessed one of the most spectacular growth overall.

Strongly linked to the success of NFTs, the outlook for the metaverse and virtual environments was already positive. However, the metaverse idea burst following Meta's renaming announcement. NFTs are digital products that are immutable assets that can be purchased or exchanged like any other piece of real estate, and they are driving a craze among investors and artists eager to cash in on the sector's fast growth.

There is now a record expansion in market development and gold rush mindset to NFTs as the fiber and backbone of the metaverse. Many

NFTs bestow certain privileges to their owners in the metaverse, such as community access and real-world value. So individuals are seeking to establish their footing inside the NFT ecosystem. Individuals will be able to buy products in the metaverse, and our current experience with their phones will appear like the beta version. The metaverse will make the feeling of owning virtual products NFTs more immersive, and you will be able to own sections of the metaverse, trade in the metaverse, connect, play, and work in the metaverse. So that is where things are going.

It is going to be a virtual overlay over our physical environment. Walmart recently confirmed its intention of joining other firms in supplying NFTs. They plan a financial transaction service using NFTs and a blockchain network that members of an online world will utilize over a worldwide computer network.

The metaverse movement has enormous potential to transform our lives and communication systems, and its growth has accelerated since the pandemic. However, the metaverse is still in its infancy, and the race has only just begun among businesses. Any firm that develops virtual and augmented reality technology, such as Magic Leap, HTC Vive, or Varjo, is a metaverse firm. A metaverse firm does psychedelic research or develops biohacking or nootropics items that affect your brain chemistry. A metaverse firm combines these two realities with dial assets.

Firms such as Meta invest in the software and technology needed to enable virtual experiences in the metaverse. Outside of a few games and popular platforms such as Decentraland, the scalability of these virtual spaces has yet to go far on the blockchain network. However, it opens up a whole new world of crypto in the form of GameFi.

Take a look at The Sandbox. This game, which appears to be inspired by Mindcraft, has its token: SAND. It was valued at $0.03 at the start of the year. It is presently valued at $2.7 and has around $2 billion market capitalization. Start purchasing and creating virtual land and assets. Get engaged in a handful of projects with 100-fold growth potential and diversify your bets.

Today's crypto investors are more likely to be experts of the metaverse. Thanks to the metaverse, the Sims might potentially be taken to a whole new level. We are genuinely constructing alternative systems of reality that will alter how we live, engage with others around the world, and do business — implying that you can hire someone in the metaverse. Meta's statement again emphasizes that the metaverse is not viewed as an 'extension' of the current internet but its successor.

While this is not entirely attributable to the metaverse, it is entirely due to cryptography: Grayscale's overall assets under management have surpassed $60 billion, surpassing State Street's STT +1.9 percent total assets under management.

How to Invest in Metaverse

The simplest method to invest cryptocurrency in the metaverse is to purchase NFTs. Graphic arts, audio, or video snippets are common NFTs that allow investors to hold a digitized asset on the blockchain network. However, there are options like stocks

Everyone knows that immediately after Meta's announcement, Decentraland's governance token Mana reached all-time highs. That was purely a momentum play, a once-in-a-lifetime opportunity for the chosen people.

Investors can invest in the Grayscale Decentraland Trust, a metaverse play on the MANA coin. Can you believe Grayscale has become a thing? Since its inception, it has increased by almost 1,000%. However, there is a catch: you must be an accredited investor, which needs investment as low as $25,000 to qualify. If anyone has invested on the first day of the fund's debut, they would have $275,000 in their account. Is this making you feel sick?

How to Get Started

One thing to note with the metaverse projects is that you may gain physical resources and assets, which can be swapped for other virtual and physical-world products. It is a crossroads of gaming and money. You have probably seen it with various blockchain projects where you can earn money just by playing games. Consider Axie Infinity (AXS), Sky Mavis's Vietnam-based blockchain network. You may earn money in NFTs and then sell them for cash.

Myobu began as a public coin in June 2021, and it is only now beginning to work on a metaverse game. They intend to release it on the blockchain in phases, beginning with a small trading card game and progressing to a full-fledged interactive role-playing game in subsequent stages. The token is accessible on Uniswap.

The establishment of metaverses will act as a catalyst for creating blockchain networks aimed at decentralized systems, decentralized finance, and smart contracts generally. There is also a different approach for investors to enter the metaverse, and investors could simply acquire the foundation builders.

It is about infrastructure-building blockchain projects that are built for smooth transfers across blockchain networks and not only blockchain systems for building decentralized apps. Polkadot is one of the most important to highlight. Polkadot aims to tackle a critical problem: ensuring interoperability across diverse blockchains on a single platform. Interoperability across blockchains will become a need in the not-too-distant future. Polkadot has a promising future in the next couple of years.

The first step is to invest in the metaverse platforms and ecosystems' foundation to benefit from these opportunities. In most cases, the token economy that underpins the ecosystem comprises shared investments. The second approach is to make a (specific) metaverse platform investment in core NFT assets. For example, it might be (gaming) accessories or luxury clothing for a virtual avatar. The third option is to purchase a social token. Because social engagement in the metaverse may lead to the creation of new social networking applications and a fan economy, it will be an important aspect of the metaverse's evolution to consider

Social Tokens

Social tokens are a form of crypto centered on a group, influencer, or business. They might be a part of the metaverse or have no connection to it. It is merely another option to diversify your cryptocurrency portfolio beyond Bitcoin, Ethereum, and the traditional altcoins like Filecoin and Litecoin. You can purchase AXS for the social component. It is absurd what we are witnessing there in terms of community development. Multibillion-dollar, player-controlled communities have now been created into games.

NFTs Brands Activities in the Metaverse

Last month, Ralph Lauren was reported to rush to open a store in the metaverse to sell virtual NFTs products as digital wear and luxury fashion. The fashion business entered the virtual environment of Roblox, which has 47 million daily active users and stocked its digital stores with virtual puffer jackets, checkered beanies, and other vintage skiwear for the winter period to be sold as NFTs.

The virtual demand for fashion and luxury products is predicted to rise from low levels, resulting in increased revenues for the sector that might reach $50 billion by 2030. The metaverse might take several years to develop; however, NFTs present a nearer-term opportunity for luxury brands.

NFTs may increase a luxury group's potential market by over 10% in eight years and increase industry profits before interest and tax by roughly 25%. Indeed, NFTs make up almost everything in blockchain-supported metaverses such as Decentraland and The Sandbox, from buildings to games to the clothing on your avatar's back. Gucci, Balenciaga, and Dolce & Gabbana are other luxury fashion brands that have begun to raise an NFT flag in the metaverse, and they will not be the last.

However, it is not only Gucci or Nike selling you an NFT of a one-of-a-kind physical world product that has been resold for more than the real-world product. Rapper Travis Scott made an estimated $20 million — including sales — in a pioneering streamed performance in Fortnite, an MMO game trying to become a metaverse.

For the 200th birthday of its founder, Louis Vuitton launched Louis The Game. Players studied the fashion brand's heritage and saw 30 NFTs, including ten by NFT Artist Mike "Beeple" Winkelmann of $69 million collage fame. Decentraland's 2021 metaverse festival included 80 artists from Nina Nesbitt and Deadmau5 to Paris Hilton. The festival also included an NFT merchandise stands, VIP sections, and a funfair with sideshow games - "come up stage and win a digital stuffed tiger NFT!"

More specifically, in a decentralized, blockchain-supported metaverse space, anybody can sell (nearly) anything, and the NFTs purchased with Decentraland's MANA native token — which serves as an in-world currency — are not limited to digital products.

More companies are exploring collaborations with esports teams, game makers, and game systems and offering special collections and components in certain games. It is an intriguing move for an industry concerned about income loss from decreased pandemic sales. Here is a chance for well-funded firms — many of which have the financial resources to weather the uncertainties of Covid-19 as smaller outlets close — to bring in revenue and users without any physical items at all.

Since the mainstreaming of NFTs, more retailers are collaborating with — or, in the instance of Nike, purchasing — businesses specializing in producing virtual clothing and virtual collectibles. Adidas is partnering with several NFT collectors and artists, including Bored Ape Yacht Club, as part of its "Into the Metaverse" effort to provide "community members" unique items and access to "virtual land experiences." These initiatives are often promoted to a growing group of bitcoin enthusiasts on the rise. Nonetheless, they are frequently commended as remarkable development by the fashion media and venture capitalists.

NFTs Trends in Virtual World

The ordinary social media user is concerned about how they look and present themselves on media. That is the gap. NFTs will be crucial to the success of bridging this gap.

Here are five NFT trends that will drive a large number of social media users to metaverse:

NFT Verification

Skeptics quickly conclude that NFTs are useless since the underlying files can be saved with a right-click. This is only a short-term issue. All major social media platforms will feature NFT verification in the coming years, and users can connect their wallets and display their verified NFTs on their profiles. Parallel to this, fingerprinting technology will enable platforms to discover and remove stolen content readily.

For Twitter, NFT-supported avatars will now appear hexagonal to distinguish them from regular profile pictures, and clicking on the NFT will take you to a page that provides NFT descriptions, including their blockchain network address and creator's identity. It is an approach for Twitter to sell subscriptions to its new premium service, Twitter Blue: a feature only available to Twitter Blue users. Only Twitter Blue users on iOS have access to the feature, which allows them to link their ethereum wallets to their Twitter accounts and see a list of their own NFTs. Users can then pick one of these images as their profile picture, including a new hexagonal border. On the other hand, Meta Facebook is yet to comment on its plans, but reports claim it is considering creating a trophy cabinet where users can show off their NFTs to friends and followers.

Incentivizing NFTs enthusiasts to showcase their collections is just another smart move by social platforms to offer users status as a service. These new digital status symbols, like conspicuous consumption of consumer goods, allow individuals to justify and showcase their membership in identity groups and social hierarchies.

Sidechains

NFT pricing will fall when sidechains like Polygon become more common. Near-zero gas expenses will also let developers incorporate greater interaction and scalability into NFTs, rendering them more social by default.

Consider Pokémon Go on the blockchain, where each Pokémon is a non-fungible token (NFT) that can be bought or sold. Every Pokémon you obtain has distinct characteristics, and you have a unique influence on how it grows through the location-based accomplishments you gain. As a Pokémon advances in level, its abilities are changed on-chain.

Music

The NFT craze of 2021 was mostly centered on visual art; however, the next frontier, which will be considerably larger in the long run, is music. Whether collecting real art or NFTs, the emotions that drive a collector's behavior are the same: they want to show one's aesthetic interests to peers; the desire to display one's identity, whether personal or collective; and, in certain situations, the urge to profit.

Although there was a lot of speculation behind the first NFT craze, self-expression and identity are the most important motivations of art collection. Music is one of the most common methods to express their inclinations and identities. TikTok began as a music video app, and music tracks continue to be an important component of videos uploaded on the network today. However, today's music is widely available, and the same tracks are available to everyone.

Assume your favorite musician publishes a one-of-a-kind 60-second music recording with a limited amount of NFTs available. You buy one and use it to produce a fantastic TikTok, and it quickly gets viral. Millions of individuals have suddenly shown an interest in using that music to create their own TikTok. However, just 100 copies are accessible everywhere. You get bids from individuals who want to purchase the music from you daily, and you may choose whether to flip it or hold it for yourself.

Wearables

Wearables are set to bring in a new age of huge expenditure on virtual products, which social media users will use to build their virtual selves, offering tremendous money-making opportunities for tech companies and investors.

Assume Kim Kardashian introduces a line of personalized AR filters — facelifts, lip fillers, cosmetics, hair, clothes, and jewelry — each one unique. If you buy one, you may wear that look solely in your TikTok videos for as long as you like, and then sell it when you are done. You can imagine the euphoria. *For more information see our extensive research into Wearable Investing in Chapter 1.*

Avatars

NFT avatars will gain dynamism, customization, and mobility. Assume you snap a selfie, and an AI creates a one-of-a-kind, personalized 3D avatar that resembles your ideal version of yourself. Bitmoji-style, but better. You may change the character's looks and poses and wear; you can make it dance, and you can make it speak in your voice simply by typing. Consider how much easier it would be to generate interesting avatars that make you feel good.

Dynamic avatars will allow for the democratization of self-expression. When Facebook initially launched, it was a little silly, but it was entertaining. When you sign in every few days, you would be notified of your friends' birthdays, view their most recent corny profile pictures, and poke them. Then came the feed, smartphones and algorithms, Instagram models, lattes, and flawlessly filtered lifestyles, and somewhere along the road, the joy gave way to a kind of social enslavement.

But, regardless of the advantages and negatives, we are already on an unstoppable march into the metaverse. We live in virtual worlds, and what metaverse allows for a richer experience in that virtual reality.

9

CRYPTOCURRENCY INVESTMENT IN THE METAVERSE

Cryptocurrencies will act as money in the metaverse space. This is based on the blockchain idea, and this is where the term "metaverse coins," "metaverse tokens," and "metaverse cryptocurrencies" come from. Tokens are used for transactions inside each metaverse project.

Numerous metaverse projects are already under development, and their coins are accessible for purchase, with some even being listed on specific cryptocurrency marketplaces. These projects are attracting the attention of both cryptocurrency investors and fans because of their potential. According to Macro, a U.K-based research group, metaverse currency gains have surpassed Bitcoin's – by a whopping 37,000 percent. Meanwhile, Bitcoin, the most valuable cryptocurrency in market capitalization, increased by 100 percent.

Metaverse projects span from digital games to NFTs exchanges, each with a distinct idea and real-world use cases. Because of the bearish market, most undervalued metaverse cryptocurrencies are presently on sale, creating an excellent investment opportunity.

Platforms such as Decentraland and The Sandbox have created virtual environments that incorporate cryptocurrency, allowing players to design and monetize structures such as virtual casinos and theme parks. The money utilized in Decentraland is called MANA, and it can be purchased on platforms like Coinbase. In Decentraland, there are even casinos where you may bet in MANA and where traders are rewarded in MANA to show up for work.

NFTs will also play a key part in the metaverse, allowing players to fully own their characters, in-game objects, and even virtual land. The greatest transaction to date was an NFT of a 259-parcel digital real estate in Decentraland, which sold for more than $900,000.

It will ultimately be possible to purchase and sell virtual products on interoperable markets from many games and worlds. So, for instance, someone may sell their virtual piece of property in the Decentraland space and use the proceeds to buy Fortnite skins. All digital products and intangible items might be represented as NFTs, making cryptocurrencies the exclusive legal currency in the metaverse. The amount of cash that gamers spend on virtual goods astounds people. Hundreds of thousands, if not millions, have been spent on virtual assets.

While no one can say for sure what the metaverse will look like or when it will emerge in its ultimate form, the role of cryptos in its development is undeniable. As we witness the advances in technology such as virtual reality and how existing industry heavyweights like Meta are becoming engaged, breakthroughs in the blockchain network and the cryptocurrency space will play an equally vital role in determining the metaverse's future.

Below are the top metaverse cryptocurrencies with a unit price of less than $9 to watch in the nearest future. They are ranked by market capitalization from lowest to highest.

Different Metaverse Cryptocurrencies

Alien Worlds (TLM)

Alien Worlds, released in December 2020, is a play-to-earn NFT game connected with the Binance Smart Chain and WAX blockchains. Participants may earn Trillium by mining and staking NFTs in the game.

Alien Worlds is an in-browser game that allows participants to create a structure using three tools and harvest the governance token trillium (TLM). The tools, which are NFTs, may be purchased through the WAX marketplace AtomicHub. Conclusion: some solutions cost less than a dollar, and more sophisticated instruments that cost a lot of money. The greater the tool's performance, the more TLM participants can mine.

Another excellent option to generate additional income with Alien Worlds is to stake Trillium on the Binance Smart Chain for durations ranging from 2 to 12 weeks and receive a bonus in TLM and a unique NFT at the end of the staking period. Players may earn anywhere from 5 to 20% in TLM for each task. TLM can be purchased on most trading platforms, including Binance, KuCoin, FTX, etc.

Chromia (CHR)

Chromia, which debuted in May 2019, is a metaverse ecosystem that makes it simple for developers to create decentralized apps. Chromia has a special software architecture that works well with Ethereum and allows developers to design apps quickly. One of the key reasons Chromia is worth keeping an eye on is that it is already home to two successful projects. Mines of Dalarnia and My Neighbor Alice are among the names in Chromia, and both games have multi-million dollar values, indicating Chromia's promise.

Chromia has a clear plan, which the group has followed. Chromia has ambitions for an Ethereum L2 base subsystem and a cross-chain communications network that will allow Chromia apps to connect with other blockchains networks. Chromia can be purchased on Binance, PancakeSwap, Crypto.com, KuCoin, and other exchanges.

CEEK VR (CEEK)

CEEK VR, which debuted in June 2018, is a metaverse project that includes a unique virtual reality headgear available at big stores such as Target and Best Buy. CEEK VR aspires to be the virtual reality music publishing and broadcasting leader. CEEK's metaverse links music artists, sports, and other online content producers to their followers. CEEK VR has world-class collaborations like Lady Gaga, U2, Sting, Ziggy Marley, and many more.

CEEK connects fans and artists through an interactive experience and allows content producers to monetize their work through the platform. CEEK enables musicians to monetize their audience by unlocking numerous revenue sources via their ERC-20 CEEK token. CEEK is available for purchase on PancakeSwap.

Metahero (HERO)

Metahero, which debuted in June 2021, serves as the doorway to the metaverse. Metahero's ultra-realistic 3D scanning system allows participants to scan themselves to achieve an entirely new level of immersion. Metahero collaborated with World Digital World, the creators of the 3D 16k modeling system utilized by CD Project, the makers of Cyberpunk 2077, to create this ultra-realistic metaverse.

Metahero aims to bring the next ten million people into the metaverse using incredibly realistic 3D avatars that look like gamers in the real world. HERO can be purchased on PancakeSwap, KuCoin, and other platforms.

WAX (WAXP)

The Worldwide Asset eXchange, aka WAX, debuted in 2017, is a blockchain network designed for metaverse and apps. WAX works particularly well with blockchain NFT games that pay you to play, and its cost structure makes WAX one of the finest blockchains for apps that require a large number of transactions.

WAX has a proof-of-stake validation system in which participants stake their WAX coins in return for CPU/NET/RAM power, allowing them to execute blockchain transactions. The WAX network makes it very easy for a newbie to utilize cryptocurrency. Furthermore, WAX contains some of the most common cryptocurrency games, such as Alien Worlds, Farmers World, and many others. WAX's AtomicHub NFT exchange is also one of the most famous on the market, making this a terrific project to keep an eye on in the metaverse. WAXP can be purchased on Binance, Crypto.com, KuCoin, and other exchanges.

Enjin Coin (ENJ)

Enjin, which debuted in June 2018, is one of the cryptocurrency industry's prominent platforms, with over 1.7 million users on its smartphone app. Enjin is a one-of-a-kind environment that provides services for brands, individuals, and developers. Enjin makes it simple to build dApps and has recently introduced its Efinity blockchain network, designed exclusively for metaverse and NFT apps. Enjin is also a prominent launchpad for many cryptocurrency projects with multi-million dollar values. Newscrypto, a reliable store for cryptocurrency news, analysis, and market signals, is a new Enjin project. ENJ can be purchased on Binance, KuCoin, Coinbase, and other exchanges.

The Sandbox (SAND)

The Sandbox is among the market's premier metaverse cryptocurrency projects, introducing its token in August 2020. The Sandbox attracted small investors after completing its alpha season one in December 2021. Consequently, this propeled it to one of the top valuable metaverse cryptocurrencies.

The Sandbox is notable for the sheer size of its platform and its high-profile collaborations with celebrities such as Snoop Dogg. The

Sandbox features one of the most popular land exchanges in cryptocurrency, with parcels trading for upwards of $10,000. The Sandbox, as one of the pioneers in metaverse space, is a necessity for any trader wanting to profit from the increase of virtual reality applications. Despite its high value, the Sandbox is immensely popular among small investors and is regarded as one of the safest options. SAND can be purchased on most marketplaces, including Binance, Uniswap, KuCoin, FTX, Gemini, etc.

Theta Network (THETA)

THETA is an advanced video and entertainment blockchain network that debuted in 2018. The THETA network contains a well-known NFT store with real memorabilia from well-known celebrities. THETA also has a streaming platform where participants may earn TFUEL tokens. THETA is preparing to introduce its new TNT-20 token TDROP in 2022. TDROP will serve as the THETA system's native token, allowing owners to define the platform's growth.

The THETA project is worth keeping an eye on in the future since its high-profile partnerships attest to the system's excellence. THETA is one of the market's top metaverse projects, making it a smart bet for the years to come. THETA may be purchased on major exchanges, including Binance, KuCoin, Crypto.com, etc.

Decentraland (MANA)

Decentraland, introduced in February 2020, is the most prominent and widely used metaverse cryptocurrency on the market. Decentraland is the longest-running metaverse in cryptocurrency, and it also has the most participants. Decentraland is free to try out, and participants may navigate their metaverse using a web browser and a compatible wallet such as MetaMask. In Decentraland, there are hundreds of events to participate in, many of which can offer you an additional income.

Decentraland's MANA, as the flagship of all metaverse cryptocurrencies and the platform with the highest valuation, may easily exceed its earlier all-time high in the upcoming metaverse bull market. For the future, it is worth keeping a watch on. MANA can be purchased on Coinbase, Binance, KuCoin, and other exchanges.

Render (RNDR)

These computer-generated environments require graphics, which necessitate a significant amount of computing power. Render is a decentralized platform that generates pictures by utilizing idle graphics processing units (GPUs). User s in the platform gain tokens and Render may supply businesses with cutting-edge graphics in an economical and scalable manner.

Wilder World (WILD)

Wilder World is a community-driven 5-D platform that holds many games and NFT-supported projects. Participants may purchase properties in Wiami, a virtual city modeled on Miami, and NFT automobiles to drive around in.

It is an intriguing initiative, but it would be great if it had a whitepaper on its website from an investor's standpoint. Furthermore, unlike the other coins on our list, Wilder World is not available in the major crypto marketplace. Nevertheless, if you are looking for less-developed metaverse coins, this is a currency to keep an eye on.

Axie Infinity (AXS)

Axie Infinity is a metaverse platform that is more closely related to the metaverse concept, but it is mostly a game. In this metaverse game, the native token is the AXS token. Axie has a market capitalization of over $5 billion, higher than any metaverse cryptocurrency. The YTD performance, on the other hand, is -20.91 percent. That may not sound encouraging to many investors, but the token's value has begun to increase again.

Even though it is built on the metaverse concept, there is no mention of virtual reality. However, it is supported by the cryptocurrency concepts of decentralization. Characters, or Axies, appear in the Axie Infinity game, and these Axies are NFTs that players may buy and sell. For example, they may create new Axies by fusing two Axies. There are also digital properties in the Axie Infinity metaverse, which might attract non-gamers as investors. A parcel, for instance, just sold for $2.3 million.

Highstreet (HIGH)

Highstreet is an intriguing metaverse project with huge promise, at least in metaverse use cases. For example, you may use the currency HIGH to buy items within this virtual world, and Shopify stores are already incorporated within the gaming system in some cases.

From a real-world — or, in this case, meta-world — standpoint, this initiative has already achieved what the metaverse space promises. This is a fantastic alternative if you are an investor that looks at practicality as a metric. The initiative is supported by HTC, which generated $5 million in August 2021. It has a market capitalization of more than $85 million as of January 2022. The coin's value has climbed by at least 90% since its launch in October 2021. It also includes gaming and has NFTs on its radar, indicating that it is up to the task of technology and cryptocurrency developments.

Floki Inu (FLOKI)

Yes, Floki Inu is another dog-meme-based coin, but it is a legitimate metaverse coin – particularly for those seeking cheap cryptos. The coin is named after Elon Musk's Shiba Inu dog, another cryptocurrency project's moniker. According to the project's site, the goal is to blend memes with real-world applications. It also claims to be launching a game and an NFT exchange. The project is still a work in progress, but that has not prevented people from purchasing FLOKI tokens. Floki Inu has no market capitalization. Since its inception in July 2021, the coin has increased by a whopping 1331.53 percent.

Terra Virtua Kolect (TVK)

Terra Virtua Kolect is a project that began in 2017 before NFTs were even developed. Nevertheless, it is now a virtual world centered on NFTs. Using the governance tokens TVK, you may generate, sell, and purchase NFTs from other users. The Terra Forma features on the platform are used to create NFTs. Because this idea is based on NFTs, it has enormous potential considering the recent boom in NFT investment. The TVK market capitalization is currently above $111 million, with a YTD performance of -16.41 percent.

Star Atlas (ATLAS)

Star Atlas is a game-based metaverse project. The game takes place in the future, in the year 2620, and allows gamers to conquer territory and acquire resources in an extremely futuristic scenario. Nevertheless, it includes a metaverse coin, ATLAS, obtained by playing the game. Consider it a typical reward-based game in which you earn tokens as you play the game and complete tasks. However, in this scenario, the benefits can generate profits.

The game is supported by Solana, which provides it with an edge over Ethereum-based projects in terms of transaction costs. It has a more than $134 million market capitalization and a YTD performance of -31.3 percent.

Epik Prime (EPIK)

Epik Prime is a metaverse cryptocurrency project based on NFTs. EPIK is a cryptocurrency that can be purchased on PancakeSwap, Uniswap, and Huobi Global exchanges. The project has also teamed with AAA Games, which has led to an increase in its value. It is a collaborative initiative with other companies to develop an NFT marketplace. Even though the governance token's uses have yet to be explored, it has already amassed a market capitalization of $62 million and a YTD performance of 129.13 percent.

Shopping in the Metaverse

Metaverse cryptocurrencies will be used for payment in many virtual environments. From buying luxury fashion to buying a digital house next door to Snoop Dogg, shopping is a key component of the systems that make up this burgeoning digital space.

But you will need money to do all of this. Here's everything you need to know to get started.

- **Get a cryptocurrency wallet**

You will be required to create a crypto wallet before you can even set up an account on metaverse networks such as Sandbox or Decentraland. This wallet will house all of your virtual money. MetaMask, which we have mentioned several times in this book, is a common wallet that can be set up using either a mobile application or a Google Chrome browser plugin. You may use your debit or credit card to convert U.S. dollars (or whatever fiat currency you are using) to crypto in the wallet. Conversion will be facilitated via crypto marketplaces like Wyre or Transak, but be aware that they will normally charge a fee.

- **Convert your cash into cryptocurrency**

Binance, Gemini, and Coinbase are some of the most popular places to acquire metaverse cryptocurrency. These exchangers will assist you in converting fiat currency into metaverse coins. You may trade your existing crypto for metaverse tokens immediately, such as Bitcoin or Ether.

Opportunity for Payment Systems

Traditional banking and payment network providers should move into the metaverse to minimize disintermediation. The traditional financial sector should adopt blockchain-based technology and aggressively seek cryptocurrency and metaverse-related collaborations and acquisitions. Conventional payment systems and payment cards will have little place on the decentralized blockchain network, so they will have to make great decisions early on to position themselves in the metaverse.

For instance, Visa's network can now convert cryptocurrency to fiat currency. According to Visa, the project is part of an initiative to simplify life for cryptocurrency firms. Visa intends to make it easier for consumers to balance their accounts on the Visa network by not forcing them to convert their crypto holdings into fiat money, such as US dollars.

Similarly, Mastercard has also announced its move to provide this feature for its customers. Mastercard's attempts follow Visa's announcement earlier that it will collaborate with 50 cryptocurrency networks on card initiatives that allow users to convert and spend virtual currency at 70 million businesses.

The distinction is made in terms of infrastructure. There is the routine of tapping a Visa card and approving transactions on the consumer side. However, most individuals have no idea what goes on behind the scenes. Money has to go between clients' banks and, say, the banks of coffee shops. Previously, cryptocurrency wallets had to convert their holdings into fiat money to send funds to Visa at the end of the day.

The cardholder's experience remains unchanged. They have a cryptocurrency balance that they can spend at a retail store. This will make it easy for more cryptocurrency wallets to provide Visa card programs to the customer. These activities also help safeguard the card-based payment mechanisms that bank issuers rely on.

Even if the metaverse does not live up to the expectations, these initiatives will almost certainly be worthwhile: Payments on the blockchain are the future way.

Metaverse Cryptocurrency Investment Tips

Small Metaverse Coins can be Difficult to Get

One challenge for investors searching for the next blockbuster metaverse coin is that many younger projects are not featured on popular exchanges. The bulk of the leading metaverse cryptocurrencies featured on CoinMarketCap is difficult to obtain in the marketplace. Smaller tokens pose a greater risk due to a lack of liquidity, increased market volatility, and a greater likelihood of project failure. Furthermore, if you want to utilize a decentralized platform, keep in mind that it may not provide the same level of security as a centralized one.

Look Before You Leap

It is usually dangerous to embark on a cryptocurrency investment just after its prices have skyrocketed. There is no certainty that the prices will remain, and it is difficult to determine the extent to which speculations have driven the prices higher.

Furthermore, many metaverse projects are underway, and we have no idea which ones will flourish. Like those in the fashion or art worlds, these trends are extremely hard to forecast, particularly if you do not utilize the platforms and are not connected to gaming and metaverse groups. However, some believe metaverses will become a multi-trillion-dollar sector in the coming years, and that cryptocurrency will play a significant role.

However, as with any crypto investment, always put in money you can afford to lose and conduct your research. Examine the management team, the project's prospects, and the size of the community. If you can utilize the product or visit the virtual environment you wish to invest in, that is much better.

10

5G AND THE METAVERSE

5G is a 5th generation wireless technology, and it can outperform 4G LTE technology in terms of speed, latency, and capacity. The increasing number of devices that can access the system is the influence of 5G on the metaverse. All connected devices can share files in real-time. While 5G is up to 20 times more efficient than 4G, it provides more benefits than simply quicker speeds. 5G speeds will enable developers in the metaverse to build apps that take full use of better response times, such as near-real-time video streaming for sports activities or security needs, due to their low latency.

5G has the potential to be extremely transformational. Replacing standard wireless methods with powerful 5G networks that enable a metaverse environment would consume far less power and perform much better.

Although the metaverse maybe all about linking immersive experience, networking in virtual space may use massive amounts of data. 5G technology, one of the most current mobile advancements, has improved in recent years, giving the power required for real-time data transmission. More importantly, consumers will be able to interact in these augmented and virtual reality experiences from anywhere, not just their homes, thanks to 5G. Returning to edge computing, increased bandwidth via 5G implies that VR rendering might be executed on an edge device and transmitted to your headset, potentially shrinking the size of virtual reality headsets in the coming years to make it more appealing for users.

5G Virtual Business Opportunities

Back in the day, infomercials swept the world. Advertising was a one-way street, with businesses hawking their products directly to consumers, with little genuine contact, possibly sending a catalog through the mail.

5G can assist retailers in driving business by enabling them to convey their stories in contexts that go well beyond the flat pages of publications and catalogs. In the age of virtual commerce, we are putting infomercials in the rearview mirror and heading straight into the epoch of virtual reality. eCommerce businesses are working hard to include 3-D images into their catalogs and push new devices to consumers.

To that end, as we get more accustomed to transacting and communicating on phones, headsets, and even our automobiles as linked devices, some of the distinctions between ordinary living and everyday commerce are being blurred. Underpinning it all is the continuous transition to 5G, the broadband cellular network standard, dramatically increasing our gadgets' capabilities. Integrating videos, images, data, and discussions into the customer experience is a factor of bandwidth.

We are now at the age where technology and devices can give those sorts of immersive experiences, implying that commerce might be all around us, thanks to livestream shopping, augmented reality, and virtual stores. The expanded capabilities should appeal to businesses and everyone interested in eCommerce and investment opportunities in the 5G network services.

The transition to 5G will be bumpy, but we will get there. However, one of the things we do not recognize and take for granted is exactly how much mobile traffic and infrastructure is traveling across the traditional bandwidths. Those previous network standards are gradually dying out and becoming less relevant to current trends and needs, though they remain dominant in many areas of the world. 5G will allow virtual reality and metaverse as a whole to be integrated into a mobile experience, whether via a smartphone or another 5G-compatible device.

We are already seeing video commerce make advances, with videos and livestreams incorporated in applications, platforms, and social media. Consumers can interact (virtually) with a sales representative to assist them with their buying experience, or they can watch a cosmetics tutorial, for instance. A virtual reality experience may "place" clothes on a physical image of the user, and we already see applications in this direction.

Due to increased bandwidth, many organizations have already begun to incorporate more interactive commerce experiences. Stores such as Crate & Barrel have provided virtual-reality technologies that allow customers to utilize augmented reality to view how furniture and other things appear in the consumer's actual living environment. This is not a piece of news, right?

The benefits for businesses are twofold: Virtual reality may help retailers enhance sales conversions while decreasing returns. It is less likely that a product will be returned if a customer can see it and how it looks before buying. There is no bound to these capabilities, so businesses can get creative to benefit from the impending shift.

The metaverse will completely embrace 3-D experiences that will expand in tandem with the availability of 5G. Retailers still have a lot of work to unlock future possibilities. When 5G becomes more prevalent, and new commerce experiences become the norm, the distinctions between real life and the virtual world will blur gradually.

Metaverse Investment Stocks

Some believe that the widespread availability of ultrafast 5G connections will be "the turning point for virtual and augmented reality. However, while smartphones allow for glimpses into the metaverse, other devices would be required to enable a more immersive metaverse experience. You will not get the best experience unless you have the actual kind of headset that allows you to connect to it.

It is still early stages, but for 5G internet providers, the emerging trend might lead to new kinds of portable, wearable devices that make extensive use of 5G connections. What 5G stocks will see an increase in value as wireless networks improve and more mobile phones, laptops, and metaverse devices adopt this technology?

According to some analysts, we are now when communications network technology as 5G wireless service providers increase their expenditure. In addition, tech giants are preparing 5G infrastructure services for different use cases.

Below is a list of different 5G stocks to look out for as the buzz of the metaverse continues.

Wireless Stocks

Apple is poised to offer AR/VR headsets by the end of 2022 or early 2023. We see this technology as a game-changer since it will allow a slew of new applications requiring high-performance hardware and faster access rates. iPhone will most likely have an upgrade cycle in fiscal 2023, driven by the demand for better connectivity, with AR emerging as the killer app for 5G. The metaverse is projected to include augmented reality and virtual reality. And Meta aspires to be a metaverse leader.

Whether years or decades away, the metaverse will allow wireless network companies to commercialize their 5G and 6G investments. Furthermore, the metaverse may provide fresh opportunities for investors in 5G and, in the future, 6G companies. 6G wireless services will allow new holographic technologies and propel augmented reality applications.

Cloud Computing Stocks

Cloud computing is likely to play a significant role in deploying 5G services. The arrival of 5G should herald the introduction of numerous new technologies that we have not yet envisioned. To make them conceivable, experts predict that cloud computing will shift from a remote cloud server to devices on the edge of a neighborhood's network.

Microsoft (MSFT) said its cloud computing division would begin offering worldwide network transport and routing services to 5G network companies. The concept was named "Azure for Operators" by Microsoft. Amazon Web Services (AMZN) and Alphabet's (GOOGL) Google also market 5G-related cloud technology and services.

Verizon has collaborated with Amazon Web Services, Google, and Microsoft to build 5G cloud services. A diverse set of technology businesses is developing 5G technology for private networks that provide business-to-business services. According to the telecom industry body 5G Americas, the potential market for incorporating 5G into private company networks will grow dramatically over the next five years, from $1.9 billion in 2020 to $16.9 billion in 2025. This indicates potential and profitable opportunities for investment. 5G infrastructure is likely to supersede Wi-Fi-based services in many industrial environments.

Chipmakers Stocks

Smartphones, virtual reality devices, and headsets are now driving most 5G chip demand from Qualcomm (QCOM), Marvell Technologies (MRVL), and others. 5G-chip producers see a lot of business from Apple, Samsung, and Chinese Android-based smartphone makers. Skyworks Solutions (SWKS) and Qorvo are also chipmakers (QRVO).

In addition to Qualcomm and Skyworks, Cirrus Logic (CRUS) and Analog Devices (ADI) manufacture semiconductors used in mobile phones. Some semiconductor manufacturers sell into the 5G network industry. Marvell, Broadcom (AVGO), Intel (INTC), Texas Instruments (TXN), and Analog Devices are among them. Meanwhile, Xilinx (XLNX) manufactures programmable chips that are integrated into prototype network gears.

Higher Frequency Airwaves Stocks

In the beginning, 5G networks will use higher frequency airwaves in metropolitan areas. Consequently, they need more equipment, cell towers, and fiber-optic cabling than in the past epoch. This is a great opportunity for the tech industry. Fiber-optic technology manufacturers also comprise the 5G wireless network distribution network. 5G networks will necessitate using "small cell" radio antennae, radio access network devices, and connections to cloud computing systems.

According to research firm Omdia, the worldwide 5G radio access market will grow to $21 billion by 2024, up from less than $4 billion in 2019. Furthermore, 5G represents a long-term potential for network equipment manufacturers.

Fiber-Optic Technology Stocks

For "long haul" applications, 5G networks will interconnect with fiber-optic networks. This will increase the dependability of developing robotics. Corning (GLW), Ciena (CIEN), and other fiber-optic firms are potential 5G stock investments.

5G is more than just faster wireless technology; 5 G offers continuous networking for individuals, computers, and devices. It is the foundation on which the metaverse will rely to build the smooth, immersive experience that we all want in our increasingly digital environment. Crown Castle manufactures "small-cell" radio antennas for urban 5G technology. Small-cell antennas, installed on utility poles or building rooftops will need fiber-optic links to local hubs. Keysight

Technologies (KEYS) develops 5G network testing equipment. In the 5G test equipment industry, Keysight competes with Viavi Solutions (VIAV) and others. These companies present huge opportunities for investments.

China may have clear advantages in the 5G metaverse race, and China is a frontrunner in 5G deployment and mobile internet technology. Last month, a government-supported 6G project led by Purple Mountain Laboratories in conjunction with China Mobile and Fudan University set a global record for real-time, 6G wireless transmission speed in a lab setting. More progress is being made through the metaverse Industry Committee, China's first official metaverse organization, which is a cooperation of China's top three telecommunications carriers — China Mobile, China Unicom, and China Telecom — and other technology businesses. They want to use their combined expertise in upcoming 6G and 5G technology design, cloud gaming, and VR technologies.

Meanwhile, NetEase is developing the necessary technologies for the sector and has formed a strategic alliance with the Sanya Municipal Government in Hainan, China's southernmost island province, to construct a metaverse-linked industrial center in the city. ByteDance has also focused its attention on building a place in China's metaverse, taking its initial steps by obtaining one of the top global VR headset manufacturers Pico last August. Nreal, a Chinese firm focusing on producing augmented reality glasses, and Besttone, a cloud gaming and entertainment business building an interconnected 5G XR platform, have made significant investments in the field.

China's lead in 5G adoption and developments in mobile internet design offer the nation an advantage in establishing the entirely virtual metaverse that Meta envisages.

Business Applications

Furthermore, 5G business use cases in smart factories and other corporate applications are expected in the nearest future. Experts predict that 5G wireless will play a role in building automation, cloud gaming, and remote health care services. Imagine the limitless opportunities that come along with gaming.

Private 5G network technologies are likely to promote new commercial uses in business. Ericsson has bought Cradlepoint, a company located in Idaho, intending to enter the 5G business-to-business sector. Enterprise solutions, particularly industrial and manufacturing, might be the major 5G revenue catalysts. Dish Network, a satellite TV provider, intends to build a 5G network in early 2022. This is another stock to be considering.

Also, AT&T said in June that it would relocate its key 5G network services to Microsoft's Azure cloud computing division. Over time, the range of 5G stocks will broaden. The metaverse, industrial Internet of Things (IoT), robotics, smart cities, and other applications will drive the future of 5G wireless. Palo Alto Networks (PANW) released new security technologies last year to protect 5G technology and web-linked industrial devices. Palo Alto's product solutions provide end-to-end 5G network security. This is a good business stock from the security point of view. The future opportunity for certain 5G stocks will be related to metaverse that blurs the barrier between mobile and fixed-line infrastructure.

11

RELATIONSHIP BETWEEN WEB3 AND THE METAVERSE

Meaning of Web3

Many individuals consider web3 to be the next phase in the evolution of the internet. It is essentially a revolution in the core foundation of the web. Nevertheless, it is crucial to note that there is no clear definition for web3, and it is still an idea under development. Tim Berners-Lee, the founder of the internet, believes that the semantic web will be the next major step in the growth of the internet.

The semantic web is concerned with making sure that all material on the web is machine-readable. People may ask, though, if virtual assistants like Alexa and Siri are currently doing the same thing. Since 2020, the concept of web3 and the metaverse has shifted dramatically, particularly with the introduction of blockchain. As a result, the emphasis of web3 has switched to the development of a decentralized web. You may be questioning why there is a need for decentralization in today's online, since everyone may connect to the internet.

However, giant IT firms own a large portion of the online, making a strong argument for a decentralized network. Aside from decentralization, web3 encompasses a slew of other notable issues, including Non-fungible tokens or NFTs, Decentralized Finance or DeFi, and Decentralized Autonomous Organizations or DAOs. Web3 is a new way to construct a new financial world. The focus of web3 would be mostly on dealing with competition from well-known platform players. It would also try to introduce new types of collaboration among online users.

Web3 and the Metaverse

Digital identity — who you are and how you present yourselves online — will become much more significant than it is now. Taking our avatars from one experience to the next will require an interoperable architecture. The feature of an avatar is one example of unbundling; new forms of virtual experiences (not only gaming, but music, art, and many other metaverse use cases) will become means of rebundling various kinds of self-expression. We will need an interoperable system for identity and property to make this reality. This is only one of the applications for Web3 in the metaverse.

Aside from that, Web3 serves as the innovative platform for the next iteration of "play-to-earn" games (P2E). P2E currently refers to some form of cryptocurrency gold-farming or power-leveling games (like in Axie Infinity). Of course, individuals have been gaming to earn for years — outside of the cryptocurrency/blockchain environment — through tournaments, Twitch livestreaming, or various types of modding games. We know that many gamers want to transform their pastime into a career, and these are examples of the emerging unbundling and rebundling that is already taking place in games.

P2E will eventually embrace all of this: not simply farming a game for currency — but also performance, creativity, competitiveness, leading, dungeon-mastering, level-designing, live roleplaying, and so on. The line between who is a gamer and who is a designer will get increasingly blurred. Bundling and unbundling will take new shapes.

For all of these revolutionary economic transactions, we require an interoperable framework of the web3.

Stocks to Buy in Web3

It is easy to dismiss Web3 as just hype with little reality. People are enthusiastic about Web3 stocks for a variety of reasons. It is primarily an opportunity to reclaim control from large enterprises in the evolving metaverse. Hence, web3 should be a step toward restoring people's power and shaping the metaverse. On that note, let us look at some Web3 stocks to consider purchasing.

However, conduct your research before making any decisions.

Nvidia (NVDA)

Nvidia company is at the forefront of almost all major technological areas. As a result, it makes perfect sense that it is at the forefront of Web3 stocks to purchase. It offers artificial intelligence, cloud computing, and deep machine learning solutions. Nvidia's technology is now used in many sectors such as communications, financial, gaming, healthcare, and other industries. There is a significant possibility that Nvidia's technology will fuel Web3 in the long run.

Nvidia reported yearly sales of $16.68 billion in the fiscal year 2021. This is a 52.73 percent increase over the previous year's total of $10.92 billion. It also earned $4.33 billion in net profits. This is a 54.94 percent increase over the $2.8 billion in 2020. So far, in 2021, Nvidia's stock is up 130 percent. It has also increased by 1,100% in the last five years.

Coinbase (COIN)

The combination of the internet, blockchain, crypto, and non-fungible tokens will be represented by Web3 stocks. Coinbase checks off two of them: cryptocurrencies and NFTs. This makes it one of the best Web3 stocks to invest in the metaverse, where cryptocurrency and NFTs will play an integral role.

Coinbase is the only publicly listed crypto company. Presently, the firm serves as a crypto marketplace where users may buy, trade, and invest in crypto. It does, nevertheless, want to create an NFT network as well. Because of its popularity, Coinbase has a decent chance of bringing NFTs into the mainstream. It is also worth noting that Coinbase is a completely remote firm. That is not to say that its staff work from home. It does not even have a real headquarters. Maybe it is now working on one based on Web3.

Coinbase reported $1.27 billion in yearly sales in 2020. This was a 143.85 percent increase over the previous year's total of $522.8 million. It also posted a $322.32 million net profit. This was also an increase of 1,160.7 percent over the previous year's loss of $30.9 million.

Block Inc. (SQ)

Block Inc. (previously Square) is a multi-faceted financial services firm. It offers point-of-sale, P2P payments systems, and crypto services. Block Inc. is one of the top Web3 stocks primarily due to its dominance. Jack Dorsey is one of Wall Street's most creative founders, and he has been dividing his time between Block and Twitter until lately. He just left Twitter to concentrate on Block Inc, demonstrating the potential in the stock. Block Inc. is expected to produce $9.5 billion by 2020, representing a 101.5 percent gain over 2019. It also posted a $213.11 million net profit.

IBM (IBM)

The IBM 5160 is a hard drive-equipped variant of the IBM PC. On March 8, 1983, the film was released. The 5100 series is widely regarded as one of the earliest home computers. When someone brings up IBM in a discussion about — well, pretty much anything — odds are the accompanying critique will center on the firm's loss of relevance. To be diplomatic, everyone who has followed IBM over the last five years understands that this is not the most realistic evaluation.

For starters, Big Blue's artificial intelligence ambitions have big ramifications for Web3 stocks. IBM can accelerate the next generation of internet connectivity by transferring more intermediate operations to AI and machine learning protocols. Essentially, it is a business proposition. Machines do not take breaks, they do not complain, and they do not wish to unionize. Interestingly, IBM has a long history with Web3, maybe longer than any other Web3 stock.

Fastly (FSLY)

Fastly is the most contentious addition to the list of Web3 stocks. On the surface, that may appear to be an odd argument. As a content delivery network service provider, Fastly brings the internet closer to the point of demand, improving performance and dependability. If you have ever wondered how your preferred websites work so smoothly practically wherever you go, a CDN is most certainly the explanation. Essentially, CDNs allow businesses to store data on their servers, reducing the distance between data and consumers worldwide.

CDNs, in some ways, reflect decentralized infrastructure. However, they are still subject to a centralized command structure, which might be a problem if a firm like Fastly fails, as it did not long ago. As a result, many "genuine" Web3 supporters are working to establish decentralized CDN alternatives.

Connectivity (TEL)

If there is one component of Web3 that outperforms previous communication technologies, it is near-complete digitization. We are rapidly approaching an environment in which everything runs on the cloud. As a result, we are increasingly detaching ourselves from the physical connection of devices.

However, our online connectivity options continue to rely on physical media. In other words, bring defective parts to the table, and Web3 stocks start to appear less appealing. Nevertheless, this is also why investors intrigued by the internet's future should pick TE Connectivity.

TE, a major provider of connectors and sensors for many sectors, is critical to the 5G deployment. Essentially, the firm supplies the physical backbone of connection solutions, allowing consumers to reap the benefits of next-generation internet without hesitation.

12

DEFI IN THE METAVERSE

Meaning of Decentralized Finance (DeFi)

DeFi refers to the network of financial apps built on the blockchain network. Decentralized finance is a project that supports open-source tools and decentralized systems to provide different financial services and goods. The goal is to build and run financial DApps on an open and trustless platform, like blockchain networks and other peer-to-peer (P2P) technologies.

Today, DeFi's three most important functions are:

- Developing financial banking services (e.g., issuance of stablecoins)
- Providing networks for peer-to-peer or pooled lending and financing.
- Enabling complex financial products like decentralized exchanges, tokenization platforms, derivatives, and futures markets

There are numerous kinds of DeFi services available within those three categories. Funding protocols, software development services, index generation, subscription payment methods, and data analysis use cases are a few more examples of services and applications. KYC, AML, and other identity management services may all be done with DeFi dApps.

When compared to the conventional banking system, decentralized finance offers various advantages. Thanks to smart contracts and distributed systems, launching a financial application or product becomes significantly less complicated and safe thanks to smart contracts and distributed systems. Many dApps, for example, are being built on top of the Ethereum blockchain, which has fewer entry hurdles and lower operational expenses. To summarize, the DeFi movement moves traditional financial goods to an open-source and decentralized environment, eliminating the need for intermediaries, lowering total costs, and significantly enhancing security.

DeFi in the Metaverse

To use the metaverse cryptocurrencies, you must first purchase them. You do so by going through a series of fiat currencies and bank third parties. But that defeats the purpose of a decentralized trading system. Decentralized finance, or DeFi, comes into play at this point. You may purchase and sell metaverse coins utilizing smart contracts, P2P transactions, and more using DeFi systems.

Proponents of a completely decentralized metaverse expected this metaverse project to emerge. For a metaverse to work ideally, there is a need for an open, trustless financial system with a high transaction rate. The metaverse also would require the storage and processing of a tremendous amount of data, which is where. NFTs as identity, as a DeFi passport, this on-chain credit score — all of these things are kind of muddled together. We can begin to see how these elements interact and prepare the stage for Web3.

The metaverse would benefit greatly from a decentralized banking system. Participants would be able to make cross-border transactions at a low cost if transactions were decentralized, and decentralized financing might help fund new and creative enterprises in the virtual environment. Because DeFi protocols already exist in the digital world, adapting them for the metaverse would be a straightforward task. Prominent banks and financial institutions will surely be looking at the metaverse, and decentralized finance still has a long way to go before competing with its centralized counterparts. Compared to the $2.3 trillion worldwide retail banking business, annualized network income for all DeFi technologies is anticipated to be $5 billion.

However, DeFi has developed significantly in just a few short years, and both regulation and the gradual stability of DeFi marketplaces will continue to drive acceptance in the coming years. DeFi might rise in the virtual environment and leave conventional banks far behind, depending on how decentralized the metaverse becomes and how much freedom participants have. It is also contingent on when the metaverse happens. The underlying software that regulates it will be published soon; therefore, it is already here. However, it is possible that the metaverse will not reach a billion people until 2031.

Regardless, decentralized finance can significantly impact the metaverse's financial sector. Many parts of the metaverse must be figured out before the idea can become a reality. Before the metaverse can materialize, many puzzle parts must come together. Casting aside the technological limitations of an "always-on" ecosystem, a Decentralized finance system involving NFTs, which we could call the "MetaverseFi," is likely to be the missing piece.

A crypto-decentralized centerpiece is essential for a metaverse's success: It requires its financial system and governance token, where value can be earned, transferred, lent, borrowed, or invested interchangeably in both a real-world or virtual environment, and most importantly, without the need for a governance system. While the metaverse may exist only in the virtual environment, I think its usage of NFTs and DeFi to bring it to life is solidly grounded in reality. The goal of an open metaverse is a compelling vision that motivates individuals and draws businesses. But if it encompasses people from China to the US, it will have to deal with the impact that growing government monitoring and control will have on DeFi.

DeFi Products in the Metaverse

Valour Inc.

Valour Inc. ("Valour"), the firm's fully owned subsidiary and a leader in virtual asset exchange-traded products ("ETPs"), has received permission to release a metaverse and gaming Index ETP. The technology company is working to close the gap between conventional financial markets and decentralized finance.

With the Metaverse and Gaming Index ETP, investors will acquire direct exposure to different metaverse-related and protocol-based initiatives with a single investment. Finansinspektionen, the Swedish Financial Supervisory Authority ("SFSA"), has given Valour permission to launch a metaverse and gaming index ETP. The ETP will include an index of the top five virtual assets connected to the metaverse, and it has received regulatory clearance to be distributed throughout EU markets.

DAOventures Metaverse Farmer

DAOventures will introduce Metaverse Farmer, the world's first DeFi metaverse Index Fund with Yield, enabling investors to benefit from the non-fungible token and cryptocurrency gaming trends. Index funds have long been a popular investment option for those seeking portfolio exposure to a wide asset category or sector. DAOventures' index fund, on the other hand, is designed on-chain and makes use of DeFi developments for added yields.

The DAOventures Metaverse Farmer (MVF) is a cryptocurrency index fund that spreads an investor's funds among a selected group of cryptos. These cryptocurrencies are native tokens for initiatives in this expanding area, Metaverse.

MVF is a smart contract-based platform built on Ethereum. ETH receives 50% of the index's weighting. The remaining half of the index is divided amongst well-known gaming ecosystems like Axie Infinity (AXS and SLP) and Illuvium (ILV). The weights and components of the portfolio were chosen based on factors like user growth and market cap. MVF lowers portfolio volatility and provides investors with extra benefits.

Everything Is Turning into A 'Fi'

As we continue to investigate this topic, keep in mind that blockchain is an essential element in the "Fi" discourse. Everything has turned into a "Fi." MachineFi, GameFi, and DeFi (obviously) are just a few of the Fi's making decentralized technology's future appear quite Fi-ne. Many significant Fi projects and experts believe that the ultimate aim is the metaverse. All of our technologies are getting increasingly networked at this time.

Future of Metaverse

On the other hand, the decentralized metaverse is intended to help the many who are in a position to enjoy the benefits of the metaverse rather than the few who hold the bulk of the network. The decentralized metaverse's success is critical for the free market and enterprises of all forms and sizes. And there is a lot the business sector can do to help balance the scales. MetaFi has many platforms to grow on and crypto investors searching for a project. What it lacks is something that many of us can provide, business. Many businesses are already reaping the rewards. Some of the most sought-after goods or services right now are those that bring blockchain into the hands of the general public. For example, the IoTeX-powered UCam blockchain-supported residential security camera recently received a CES innovation award, and StarCrazy is one of the most popular metaverse Play2Earn games on the market. These two enterprises have one thing in common: they both participate in the decentralized metaverse and profit from it.

CONCLUSION

Digital technology has altered how we view the world over the last two decades, providing unrestricted access to information and broadening our social interactions. Nevertheless, the next technological advancement, the metaverse, will most likely be more immersive. Thanks to increased processing power, quicker internet access, and other technical developments such as artificial intelligence and machine learning, tech businesses can create virtual worlds. These venues are designed to offer users a feeling of being present without requiring them to leave their current location.

In the future, people will be able to transfer themselves as avatars to virtual worlds to work, play, buy, work out, study, and experience most aspects of life virtually. Participants may also use complex graphics to recreate real-life aspects like their home or business environment, such as a beach in Hawaii. It is worth noting that virtual worlds are not a new concept. Virtual reality environments have been running for years thanks to Nintendo, Decentraland, The Sandbox, and Roblox (RBLX). These businesses collectively draw millions of users to the virtual environment. The stakes are enormous for huge tech corporations, who want to integrate these various groups into a unified metaverse. They are bound to get a piece of the billions of dollars at risk by achieving this goal. The worldwide income from virtual gaming alone might reach $400 billion by 2025, up from $180 billion now, a 122 percent rise.

Our social lives and gaming combine and generate a big, fast-growing digital products consumer market. Content providers and other players utilize crypto to sell virtual products in the metaverse economy. This new frontier allows participants to own their digital products as NFTs exchange them, resulting in a complete new free-market internet-native economy that can be monetized in the real world. And many major corporations are beginning to participate. Real estate investments are also becoming more accessible due to the metaverse economy.

Some individual investors may already have significant access to the metaverse since many significant U.S. public corporations are either engaging in the technology or actively trying to invest in it. And today, the gaming industry is the most dynamic and engaging category in entertainment across all networks. Gaming will play a vital role in the development of metaverse space.

Most investors are familiar with cryptocurrencies, NFTs, DeFi, Web3, and other digital technologies. Nonetheless, many of these investments come with more risks and volatility than traditional investing. As a result, it is critical to think about your risk tolerance, conduct your research, and be comfortable with the amount of money you are willing to lose. A varied portfolio with many great assets is sensible to profit from this tremendous opportunity.

Dear reader,

As independent authors reviews are often difficult to come by. Please leave a review on the platform where you bought this book.

Many thanks,
NFT Trending Team

JOIN OUR

FIRST READER REVIEW

TEAM

HERE:

mindsetmastership@gmail.com

9 781915 002136